YORK NOTES

Samuel Taylor Coleridge
Selected Poems

Note by Richard Gravil

 Longman   York Press

The right of Richard Gravil to be identified as Author of this Work has been asserted by him in accordance with the Copyright, Designs and Patents Act 1988

YORK PRESS
322 Old Brompton Road, London SW5 9JH

PEARSON EDUCATION LIMITED
Edinburgh Gate, Harlow,
Essex CM20 2JE, United Kingdom
Associated companies, branches and representatives throughout the world

First published 2000
Fourteenth impression 2015

ISBN: 978-0-582-42480-7

Designed by Vicki Pacey
Phototypeset by Gem Graphics, Trenance, Mawgan Porth, Cornwall
Colour reproduction and film output by Spectrum Colour
Produced by Ashford Colour Press Ltd., Gosport, Hampshire

CONTENTS

PART ONE

INTRODUCTION

HOW TO STUDY A POEM

Studying on your own requires self-discipline and a carefully thought-out work plan in order to be effective.

* First, learn to hear it: say it aloud, silently, whenever you read it. The poem lives in its sounds; poetry is as close to music and dance as it is to prose.
* A poem is not reducible to what you can extract from it at the end of the process of interpretation; it is a dramatic event, a *sequence* of thoughts and emotions.
* The only true summary of the poem is the poem. What can be summarised is one's experience of the poem, the process by which one arrives at a reading.
* What is the poem's tone of voice? Who is speaking?
* Does the poem have an argument? Is it descriptive?
* Is there anything special about the poem's language? Which words stand out? Why?
* What elements are repeated? Consider **alliteration**, **assonance**, **rhyme**, rhythm, **metaphor**.
* What might the poem's **images** suggest or symbolise? Do they fit together thematically?
* Is there a regular pattern of lines? Are they end-stopped (where the grammatical units coincide with line endings) or does the phrasing 'run over'?
* Can you compare and contrast the poem with other work by the same poet?
* Finally, every argument you make about the poem must be backed up with details and quotations. Always express your ideas in your own words.

This York Note offers an introduction to the poetry of Coleridge and cannot substitute close reading of the text and the study of secondary sources.

The one thing everyone knows about Coleridge is that he took opium in nearly lethal quantities and that he wrote a handful of really fine poems. Among these are *The Ancient Mariner*, with its vivid, spell-binding narrative of crime and purgatory, 'Kubla Khan', a haunting narcotic dream, and *Christabel*, a **Gothic** narrative so disturbing that Coleridge could not finish it. For each of these poems Coleridge employed a brilliantly original form and metre. They *sound* like nothing before them, or since, and run over with intensely imagined **imagery**.

Also, long before the so-called 'confessional' poets of the 1950s and 1960s, he invented the popular idea that poetry should be an analysis of the writer's psyche. Although the poet must be 'aloof from his feelings', in the sense of being able to look at himself as a third person, the most interesting poetry, he himself said, is that in which the poet 'develops his own feelings'. In 'Frost at Midnight' he admits the reader into his fireside hopes, seeming to making poetry out of the immediate, anxious or pleasurable moment, while such poems as 'The Pains of Sleep', and the 'Letter to — [Sara Hutchinson]' are strewn with gobbets of raw experience, revealing, as one critic has said, 'the full throb of Coleridge's unhappiness'. In fact, a sharp sense of the nakedness of the human soul, whether in ecstasy or in anguish, is present in much of his poetry, whether narrative or confessional. The dream of 'Kubla Khan', the sufferings of the Mariner, the ambiguous dreads of *Christabel*, are as revelatory of Coleridge as the devastating self-analyses of 'Dejection' and 'The Pains of Sleep'. Coleridge's poetry is Romantic because he was capable of such heights and depths of feeling, but had he not also been a great poet and superb technician his torments would not have become significant.

Coleridge also wrote so directly and powerfully about the politics of his day. As a young man, he was energetically promoting a commune in America for like-minded friends, which he called 'an experiment in human perfectibility', writing dazzling anti-war journalism, and demonstrating considerable courage by lecturing against the slave trade in Bristol, the heart of British slaving. So, however remote some of his quietly meditative poetry may appear from political concerns, its motifs of escape and retreat and refuge are themselves indicative of someone writing in a period of turmoil and dissent.

Equally, the assertion of many of his poems that God is in nature

and that both God and nature are in love with human liberty are
themselves political statements. Indeed the very prominence of nature in
his early poetry, at a date when the phrase 'the system of nature' was pan-
European code for republican and rationalist hostility to priests and
kings, is provocative. His earliest long poem, 'Religious Musings', overtly
welcomed the French Revolution as signs of the final overthrow of
monarchy, priestcraft and of property itself.

1793 Many see Coleridge as a man of immense and varied talents who
frittered away his life in a series of brilliant gestures – in poetry,
journalism, political and religious writings, and, above all, talking – and
left no substantial work in any of these fields. Coleridge, in part, created
this myth of himself as a creature of disappointing achievement, and
when he died, most of his contemporaries regarded him as a brilliant
failure, having taken him at his word. This is an illusion. The *Collected
Coleridge*, when it is complete, will show an astonishing output in
journalism, lectures, poetry, plays, philosophy, criticism, huge volumes of
marginalia, autobiography, table talk and voluminous notebooks.
Certainly, compared with his aspirations, his published achievement was
fragmentary: but his fragments already dwarf the organised output of
many of his more organised contemporaries.

When, in an effort to escape his addictions and provide for his
family, Coleridge set sail for Malta in 1804 to take up a diplomatic post
as Public Secretary to the Governor of Malta, his old friend Humphry
Davy, of the Royal Institution, wrote to him: 'You must not live much
longer without giving to all men the proof of power, which those who
know you feel in admiration.' A year later he was exploring Rome with
Washington Allston, a young painter from South Carolina, who looked
back on him as the most prolific mind he encountered in that bohemian
environment. He wrote: 'meet him when or where I would, the fountain
of his mind was never dry [and] I am almost tempted to dream that I
once listened to Plato in the groves of the academy'. John Stuart Mill, the
most eminent British philosopher of the nineteenth century, saw
Coleridge as one of the two seminal minds of the age, the other being
Jeremy Bentham, the founder of Utilitarian philosophy. And for
Wordsworth who once described him poetically as 'a fountain at my door
whose only business was to flow' he was, simply, 'the most *wonderful* man
I ever knew'.

PART TWO

SUMMARIES

Coleridge's poems were published in various volumes during his lifetime, principally, Poems on Various Subjects *(1796),* Lyrical Ballads *(1798),* Sybilline Leaves *(1817) and* Poetical Works *(1828). The standard edition (prior to the forthcoming Bollingen* Poetical Works *edited by J.C.C. Mays), is* The Complete Poetical Works of Samuel Taylor Coleridge, *edited by E.H. Coleridge, Oxford University Press, Oxford, 1912, which is available in paperback. All the poems discussed in this Note are included in* Samuel Taylor Coleridge: Poems, *edited by John Beer, Everyman's Library, 1993, which has excellent introductions to each of its sections. All except the 'Letter to —* [Sara Hutchinson]' *are also in* The Portable Coleridge, *edited by I.A. Richards, Penguin Books, 1977, which includes letters and prose extracts. All are in* Samuel Taylor Coleridge: Selected Poems, *edited by H.J. Jackson, Oxford World's Classics, 1999. This York Note follows the World's Classics edition, though dates given for poems sometimes vary.*

DETAILED SUMMARIES & COMMENTARIES

SONNET: TO THE RIVER OTTER 1793

As the poet addresses the stream which gives its name to his birthplace, Ottery St Mary, he remembers scenes of his childhood

The poet apostrophises his 'native brook', blending his reminiscences of the appearance of the stream, and the pleasures he associates with it, with references to his present state of manhood. One particular memory, that of skimming flat stones along the surface of the water counting how many times they bounce, links the first and second **quatrains**. So great was the pleasure of this activity, it is implied, that whenever in later years the poet closes his eyes on a sunlit scene the waters of the Otter rise in memory.

Y

The way the poet is taken back into childhood seems to be signified in the opening address to 'river', 'brook', 'streamlet', each term being more diminutive than the last. Are the 'light leaps' of the stone just an accurate image, or do they represent the leaps of imagination? The **metre** in the last line seems also to echo the skimming leaps of smooth thin stone, even while it implies that the poet is no longer carefree. Even the rhyme scheme is sinuous in the way it avoids using an obvious pattern of repeated quatrains: it rhymes *abba acdc dcdece*.

the West the counties of Devon, Cornwall, Somerset and Dorset
vein'd with various dyes a reference to the different rock strata making up the sandy bed of the river

RELIGIOUS MUSINGS 1794–6

In a Christmas Eve meditation, the poet interprets the conflict between Revolutionary France and the Monarchical powers of Europe as foretelling the Second Coming of Christ and the era of universal peace

Coleridge's own summary of this long and difficult poem was very brief: 'Introduction. Person of Christ. His prayer on the Cross. The process of his doctrines on the mind of the Individual. Character of the Elect. Superstition. Digression to the present War. Origin and Uses of Government and Property. The present State of Society. The French Revolution. Millennium. Universal redemption. Conclusion.'

The poem treats the character of Christ as a symbol of the Invisible (i.e. God). God is 'Nature's essence' (line 48) and those who love the Creator care nothing for 'created might' (lines 64–5), that is, monarchs and their hirelings. Belief in God 'fraternises man' (line 129). From a brief survey of the immediate political scene (lines 160–81) the poet passes to a review of the rise of property (line 204) and want (line 214). God's purposes have, however, been revealed by the heroes of science and truth, especially Benjamin Franklin, America's 'patriot Sage' (line 234) and Joseph Priestley, England's 'patriot, and saint and sage' (line 371). The present political convulsions show that 'the hour is nigh' (line 308). Kings and Captains will be cast down, time will cease, and the **Millennium**, the 1,000-year rule of Christ and his Saints, will begin.

Coleridge celebrates the **Unitarian** view of history as progressing towards the victory of science and truth over error and mystery. Did Coleridge really believe that 'The Lamb of God hath opened the fifth seal' (line 304) and that the apocalyptic end of history promised in the book of Revelation was about to take place? In a symbolic sense at least, this was believed by Coleridge's intellectual heroes at this date – including William Frend (a Cambridge tutor persecuted for his beliefs) and Joseph Priestley (1733–1804) discover of oxygen and radical thinker on science, politics and religion.

THE EOLIAN HARP   AUGUST 1795

> **In a relaxed mood of courtship, the poet's mind is seduced into speculations from which he is saved by his love for Sara, his fiancée**

The Aeolian (or Eolian) harp, a seventeenth-century invention, consisted of tuned strings stretched over a sounding-box. Aeolus was god of the winds: the harp was placed in a window where it responded to the changing breeze with sequences of chords, as though Aeolus were playing it. Coleridge represents himself and Sara Fricker, a few weeks before their marriage, sitting in their garden at dusk and listening to this music – the music of nature. The lute, or harp, is first described as emblematic of a yielding maid, reproving her lover – the caressing wind. Then its music suggests, more fancifully, the bewitching sounds of elves, and melodies which seem to hover like birds of paradise. Lines 26–33 were added to the poem as an afterthought in 1817: they express Coleridge's occasional sense of the harmony between the soul and all creation – 'O the one life within us and abroad' – in which joy is the common element of all life, and even the 'still air/ Is Music slumbering'.

In the second verse paragraph, beginning 'And thus, my love!', the poet compares the sounds made by the wind on the harp to the thoughts crossing his brain as he idly watches the sun's reflections on the distant sea at noon. Such thoughts come and go like the natural breeze. One such thought now comes to him: what if all life is subject in the same way to 'one intellectual breeze/ At once the Soul of each, and God of All?' At line 49 Sara's expression seems to disapprove of such speculations, and the poem ends very contritely.

The sudden change at line 49 may seem inexplicable. The idea of God's presence in nature is an attractive one, after all. But Coleridge identifies it immediately as a **Pantheistic** thought. He is in danger of attributing all his thoughts, which may be erroneous, to God; if his thoughts are God thinking in him, he has no free will, and is incapable of sin. So the final verse paragraph makes amends for the idle heresy with numerous expressions of piety. Sara's meekness, mildness and humility as a 'Meek daughter in the family of Christ' show his own thoughts to be 'Dim and unhallowed' (unholy). He rejects his fine thought as a creation of the 'unregenerate mind' and of the ever-babbling spring of 'vain Philosophy'. He knows that he must not identify with God, but give thanks for God's gifts – peace, his cottage and Sara. At the beginning of the poem these were all, unproblematically, 'ours'. Many readers may feel more impressed by the beauty of the first section, or the soaring thought of the second, than by the piety of the third. But the poem expresses a genuine intellectual drama in which Coleridge's speculative mind finds itself in conflict with his Unitarian faith.

Is the erotic language of the opening section – with the phallic lute placed lengthways in the vaginal casement, leading to those delicious surges – a sign that his bodily feelings are as licentious as his thought will become? (Critics sometimes call this a honeymoon poem, but the couple are engaged, not married, and Coleridge associated sexual licence with atheism).

The way the last line recalls the opening images of 'Peace, and this cot, and thee', but now in a very different frame of mind, is a characteristic pattern in Coleridge's later meditative poems.

sequacious successive
the main poetic term for the sea
Plastic forming, moulding

unregenerate unreformed, unspiritual
Wildered bewildered, both in the sense of 'mentally confused', and in the older sense of 'exiled into wilderness'

THIS LIME-TREE BOWER MY PRISON 1797

Since nature is omnipresent, so are love and beauty. There is no such thing as solitude. Nature is a medium through which distant friends are united

Coleridge finds himself imprisoned in his neighbour's garden, while his friend Charles Lamb (to whom the poem is addressed) is, in Coleridge's view at least, enjoying a brief liberation from the great city (this is poetic licence: Lamb loved London). The disappointment expressed in the opening lines is very intense: Coleridge is missing a walk with one of his oldest friends and two of his newest. Having told them to visit a particular spot ('that still roaring dell, of which I told'), he follows them in imagination, first recreating the scene in precise detail, and then participating imaginatively in their enjoyment. He knows that emerging from the shade of the dell, his friends will next rejoice in the distant view of the sea. Imagining Lamb in this scene, Coleridge desires for him a rich sunset, for his friend is in need of the restorative joy that accompanies such sights. But in desiring a **sublime** experience for Lamb, Coleridge himself is overcome by joy, which now spills over into the scene where he sits 'imprisoned'. The bower itself is filled with radiance, and with interest, in consequence of his own sense of joy. At the close of the poem Coleridge and Lamb are pleasingly united by the homeward flight of the 'last rook' at evening.

Like many of Coleridge's poems this one emerges from a community of friends. The **imagery** of the 'long lank weeds' is taken quite directly from Dorothy Wordsworth's journal, and the occasion of the poem is described by Coleridge in a letter to Southey: 'Charles Lamb has been with me for a week – he left me Friday morning. The second day after Wordsworth came to me, dear Sara accidentally emptied a skillet of boiling milk on my foot, which confined me during the whole time of Lamb's stay and still prevents me from all walks longer than a furlong.'

By using the term 'prison', Coleridge is reminding himself of the belief he expressed elsewhere (in a poem called 'The Dungeon', for instance) that the ministrations of nature can transcend any such imprisonment, and reminding his readers, perhaps, that in the 1790s such opinions can land you in jail. Another visitor this year was John Thelwall, the notorious agitator who was also a great walker (walking was a suspiciously democratic activity!) and who had been in prison for his democratic opinions. He spent his imprisonment writing poems in a not dissimilar conversational style.

In its subtle and convincing shifts of feeling, and its use of natural, colloquial speech rhythms, this is the first of Coleridge's wholly successful 'conversation poems'. It is relatively free of the conventional emblems and **allegory** used in his earlier poems, and of formal **poetic diction**. There is, however, an awkward (perhaps deliberately clumsy?) double-negative in lines 45–6 ('Nor ... have I not marked'). The imperatives in lines 32–7 (where he is telling each element of the landscape what to do, as if he were conducting an orchestra, as in 'richlier burn, ye clouds!', etc.) may strike you as too formally **rhetorical** to suit the new conversational style of the rest of the poem. Or do they convey the strength of his desire that Lamb should experience a moment of sublimity?

The moralising note is less obtrusive in this poem than in 'The Eolian Harp', although it is present in lines 59–67 (and perhaps in his choice of the 'humble bee' to illustrate contented nature in line 58). On the other hand, you may feel that there is a difference between the *new* Romantic morality of lines 60–64 and the *old* morality of 65–7. Does the act of 'blessing' the rook remind you of the similar event in *The Ancient Mariner*? In this happy mood even the 'creaking' of the rook's feathers – not a conventionally beautiful sound – contributes to the harmony of the scene.

springy 'elastic, I mean', said Coleridge in a letter to Southey
long lank weeds Adder's Tongue. Coleridge copied the imagery here from Dorothy Wordsworth's account of the dell in her journal
some fair bark poetic diction for almost any kind of boat

evil and pain/ And strange calamity the previous year, in a fit of insanity, Charles's sister Mary had stabbed their mother to death. Charles, too, had periods of mental instability, although he was normally the happiest and most gentle of Coleridge's friends

usurps encroaches upon

FIRE, FAMINE, AND SLAUGHTER: A WAR ECLOGUE 1797–8

The poet attributes atrocities in France to the machinations of Prime Minister Pitt

Like the witches in Shakespeare's *Macbeth* the spirits of Fire, Famine and Slaughter meet in the French region of La Vendée to discuss their recent doings. Slaughter has drunk the blood of 'thrice three hundred thousand men'; Famine has devoured their wives and children; while Fire has been destroying the farms and cottages of Ireland. Each spirit claims to have been let loose by Pitt ('Letters four do form his name') whose name they will not speak because it causes riotous glee in hell.

William Pitt the Younger was widely blamed for provoking royalist uprisings in La Vendée and thus bringing on the worst excesses of the Terror. Writers as diverse as President Jefferson and William Wordsworth in *The Prelude* held Pitt, rather than Maximilien Robespierre, responsible for the repressive policies of the revolutionary Directory. Ireland is brought in because of equally brutal repression of the 1798 rising in Ireland. Percy Bysshe Shelley's 'A Masque of Anarchy' used a similarly vitriolic style to attack British repression in 1819.

FROST AT MIDNIGHT   FEBRUARY 1798

The poet travels back in a train of associations from his anxious present as a new parent, to his lonely schooldays, and his own infancy, and then forward to the imagined future of his infant son, who will grow up enjoying nature as the language of God

Like 'This Lime-Tree Bower', this poem has a precise situation. Coleridge is speaking as a parent. His child, Hartley (now about eighteen months old) is sleeping, and in the context of a delicately sketched night scene Coleridge pursues a train of thought. The frosty calmness of the night is tangible, vexing the poet's meditation. All the 'goings-on of life' are 'inaudible as dreams'. Even the flame of the fire is still. Two things only are 'unquiet': the film of soot or ash fluttering on the grate, responsive to the otherwise imperceptible currents of air, and felt by the poet as an image for his own 'unquiet' soul.

The 'film' takes him back to his own childhood, when he believed in the superstition that this phenomenon foretold a visit from an absent friend (see Coleridge's footnote: note 87), so that he would spend the following day expecting a visitor from home. The phrase 'Dear Babe' recalls us to the poet's present situation and feelings, but also links the poet's childhood with his son's.

He now looks forward to Hartley's boyhood, as he has looked back on his own, and prophesies that Hartley's will be very different – not 'pent' (imprisoned) among cloisters in the city, as Coleridge and Lamb were, but free as a breeze to roam the countryside, being educated by the 'lovely shapes and sounds' of nature which are the language of God.

The last movement, or verse paragraph, first imagines the seasons to come, summers alternating with winters, and then returns us to the present scene – the snow, the thatch, the silences when the wind is in a trance – preparing for the repetition of the opening theme. Now the 'secret ministry' of frost is making icicles 'Quietly shining to the quiet Moon'.

It is worth analysing very carefully the **alliterations** and **assonances** in the first paragraph: this is not obviously musical poetry, but its effects are carefully managed.

Although the third movement foretells a childhood for Hartley which will be much like Wordsworth's, there is a religious emphasis rarely present in Wordsworth's poetry.

The close of the poem is not only an excellent example of Coleridge's way of bringing the conversation poems full circle but one of the most intriguing examples of symbolism in his work.

See also Extended Commentaries, Text 2. Before reading that, ask yourself what is symbolised in the icicles.

vexes usually 'annoys', but here 'stirs' or 'moves'
freaks caprices, vagaries
presageful full of presentiments
preceptor (archaic) teacher
playmate ... clothed alike that is, when both wore baby-clothes

France. AN ODE FEBRUARY 1798

The poet's reason for welcoming the French Revolution in 1789 and condemning it in 1798 is that, unlike France, he is unchanged in his devotion to 'divinest liberty'

This poem was directly inspired by the French invasion of Switzerland. The first stanza, as Coleridge explains in the prose 'Argument' which is included in some editions (see note 89), is 'An invocation to those objects in Nature the contemplation of which had inspired the Poet with a devotional love of Liberty'. The second stanza describes his 'exultation' at the start of the Revolution, and 'his unqualified abhorrence of the Alliance against the Republic'. The third stanza explains his initial willingness to excuse French atrocities (during the 'Reign of Terror'), and his continuing belief that the revolution would lead to liberation elsewhere. The fourth stanza begs forgiveness for having so long supported the butchers who have now invaded Switzerland, and tainted 'the bloodless freedom of the mountaineer', while the fifth reaches the conclusion that ideal of freedom cannot possibly be realised 'under any form of human government'.

The poem is *addressed* at start and finish to 'Ye Clouds, ... Ye Ocean-Waves ... Ye Woods'. Is there any part of this stanza that you find surprising? Why, in the second stanza, does he make so much of his enthusiasm for the French revolution? Is there any indication in this stanza of the repudiation he is about to make?

Coleridge's prose summary of the final stanza explains that the ideal of Freedom, which 'the mind attains by its contemplation of its individual nature, and of the **sublime** surrounding objects [the works of nature]', does 'not belong to men, *as a society*'. How would you interpret this claim?

Y

See Extended Commentaries, Text 1.

sensual, dark those limited to their senses, unenlightened by intellect or Reason

patriot ... toils at this date patriot meant 'lover of the people' and toils meant 'snares'

Priestcraft's harpy minions rapacious (greedy) servants of the priesthood

FEARS IN SOLITUDE

Written in April, 1798, during the Alarm of an Invasion

The poet knows that his country's own corruptions and militarism merit punishment, yet scorns the invader, and pleads that the innocent must not suffer for the sins of their rulers

LINES 1–28

The poet takes evident delight in describing his 'spirit-healing nook', a place loved above all by such men as can enjoy 'influences' from the lark, the sun and the breeze, making out of these a 'meditative joy' and finding 'Religious Meanings in the forms of Nature'.

LINES 29–86

His calm is, however, disturbed by thoughts of his fellow men and the possibility that some are already engaged in repelling an invasion. He sees this possibility as too well deserved by a country which has itself invaded others, and whose ruling institutions are a club for 'mutual flattery'. The land is polluted by wealth and God has been forgotten (here Coleridge is performing the role of a biblical prophet).

LINES 86–129

The nation is guilty of having welcomed war with France, as long as the fighting is done abroad. Even women and children find the news of war exciting, and seem unaware of its cruel realities, 'As if the soldier died without a wound'. What if Providence should decide to teach these thoughtless people the meaning of the words they use so lightly?

LINES 129–52

He prays, however, that innocent women and children will be spared, and calls on his pure countrymen to repel the 'impious foe'. The French have no right to invade. Let Englishmen win, but in a spirit of repentance.

LINES 153–97

Political strife divides people into two camps: naïve radicals who blame all social ills on the government, rather than themselves, and the ruling class who call their critics traitors or the enemy within. Such accusations have been levelled at him, but he refutes the charge of disloyalty in a lyrical expression of patriotic feeling.

LINES 198–235

He hopes that the emergency will pass away like the gust of wind that has just 'roared and died away/ In the distant tree', too distant to bend the delicate blades of grass at his feet (symbolising the ordinary people who are too often the victims of war?). Walking home he has a glimpse of the sea and of an expanse of fields and trees. The domestic peace he has enjoyed in Stowey becomes an **image** of a better future for the land.

'Fears in Solitude' has been called one of the best political poems in the language. Written 'during the Alarm of an Invasion', it is a meditation composed of observations of nature, anxieties about the possibility of a French invasion, strong criticism of national corruptions, a resurgence of patriotic feelings, and thoughts on the meaning of liberty. It has something of the circular structure of the conversation poems of 1797–8, beginning and ending with reference to Coleridge's quiet life at Nether Stowey. Unlike the other conversation poems, however, this one is addressed to the nation (O Britons! O my brethren!) and like other political poems (Yeats's 'Easter 1916' for instance) it is also about the birth of a new sense of personal identity.

Equally, however, it about the birth of an *ideal* identity, a Coleridge with Wordsworth's mountain upbringing and firm character, who has derived ennobling thoughts from 'lakes and mountain-hills' (line 184) or a Wordsworth with Coleridge's religious feeling who finds '*religious* meanings in the forms of nature'. The man described in lines 14–16 is like both of them in having known enough youthful folly (e.g. excusing Robespierre's Terror?) to make 'his early manhood more securely wise'.

Is Coleridge's penitence a little smug? How often does the term 'we' actually include 'I'? At line 42 'We have offended very grievously' is so vague as to be inclusive, but does he include himself in the 'we' who have enslaved distant tribes (line 50)? or 'drunk … Pollutions from the brimming cup of wealth' (line 60)? or 'loved / To swell the war-whoop' (line 89)? And what blend of penitence and self-vindication makes up lines 160–71? The claim that 'There lives nor form nor feeling in my soul / Unborrowed from my country' (lines 192–3) is a touching act of identification with his countrymen, yet it contrasts with the new importance attached to 'solitary musings'. You should compare this poem with the 1795 'Reflections on having left a Place of Retirement' in which Coleridge describes leaving his 'valley of seclusion' to play his part in the struggle for progress. At that time he thought it selfish to stay in the marital cottage at Clevedon nursing his conscience, instead of committing himself to the political arena. Now Nether Stowey seems an ideal place to engage in 'solitary musings' and 'thoughts that *yearn* for humankind'.

Nevertheless, as a set of poems, 'France. An Ode', 'Frost at Midnight' and 'Fears in Solitude' are perhaps unified by the blend of domestic virtues and active benevolence which at this point in history – caught between French terror and British 'war-whoops' – dissenting radicals were promoting as the moral high ground.

the Book of Life the Bible
or … or either … or
the mansion of my friend Tom Poole's house in Nether Stowey

KUBLA KHAN: OR, A VISION IN A DREAM. A FRAGMENT 1797–8; 1816

The poet tells of an opium dream about the building of
Kubla Khan's pleasure dome in Xanadu, and a woman
wailing for her demon lover. If only the poet could
remember another dream, of a damsel with a dulcimer, he
would build that dome in air, for all to see

INTRODUCTION
The poet narrates the circumstances of the composition of his poem
According to the poet he took an 'anodyne', and, while reading from a
travel book, fell asleep over the words 'here the Khan Kubla commanded
a palace to be built, and a stately garden thereunto. And thus ten miles of
fertile ground were inclosed within a wall'. (The actual words in Purchas's
Pilgrimage, 1613, are: 'In Xamdu did Cublai Can build a stately Palace
…'). He dreamed that he had composed 200–300 lines of poetry without
conscious effort, but while writing out these lines he was interrupted, by
'a person on business from Porlock' and found afterwards that he could
recollect only 'eight or ten scattered lines and images'. Since then he has
frequently wished to 'finish for himself what had been originally given to
him'.

VERSES 1–36
A dream of Kubla Khan's stately pleasure dome, amid gardens, a
romantic chasm, a sacred river and a sunless sea
The Khan decrees a 'pleasure-dome' where the river Alph plunges
through caves to an underground sea. A wall is built to enclose a fertile
paradise of gardens, streams and groves. The second paragraph
introduces the contrasting works of nature, the 'deep romantic chasm'
which is both 'savage' and 'holy' – a fitting place for a story in Romance.
The force of water is described in terms which suggest turmoil, erosion
and fertility all at once. The river meanders for five miles before it reaches
the caverns and disappears in tumult, amid which tumult Kubla hears
'ancestral voices prophesying war'. In a last fleeting glimpse the dome is
reduced to a 'shadow', and the entire scene is represented in terms of
paradox: the 'mingled measure' of fountain and caves, and the devised
'miracle' of 'A sunny pleasure dome with caves of ice'.

VERSES 37–54

The poet remembers a previous vision concerning an Abyssinian maid whose song, if he could remember it, would enable him to 'build that dome in air'

There is a clear break at this point. The narrator turns from his fading dream to an entirely different vision, of an Abyssinian damsel with a dulcimer, whose song, if he could remember that, would not only enable him to rebuild Kubla's dome (or his dream of Kubla's dome) but give him the reputation of a prophet inspired by the milk and honey of paradise.

A manuscript of the poem includes this brief comment: 'This fragment with a good deal more, not recoverable, composed, in a sort of reverie brought on by two grains of opium taken to check a dysentery, at a Farm House between Porlock and Linton [on the North Devon coast], a quarter of a mile from Culbone Church, in the fall of the year, 1797.' The poem was probably finished in 1798, and was not written 'instantly' as the longer note claims.

Which part of the poem is the Vision and which is the Dream? Are visions truer than dreams? Is all the poem a fragment, or only the dreamed part? Is it 'really' a fragment, or could it be a complete work in the fragment genre?

Before reading Extended Commentaries, Text 3, accept this poem's invitation, and allow its **images** and symbols to form significant clusters in your mind. Listen to Coleridge's strange West-Country orientalism (he was a Devon lad, with life-long Cornish and Somerset friends, staying in a Devon farmhouse, high on a drug he had used since childhood, and if he dreamt this poem he dreamt in a Devonshire accent, so the 'a' assonances in Xanadu and Khan are full rhymes with 'ran' and 'man').

Purchas Samuel Purchas, 1575–1626, edited several works of religious history and journals of great explorers

Kubla Khan ... ancestral voices ... war it is unclear whether Coleridge knew that the historical Kubla was credited with introducing Buddhism to his warlike culture as a result of a vision. Kubla's grandfather, Genghis Khan, extended his empire as far as central Europe; Kubla's attempt to conquer

Japan was defeated by a typhoon which destroyed his fleet (just as the Russian winter defeated Napoleon?)

Alph a contraction of Alpheus, a river mentioned in classical texts as having prolonged underground sections, and associated with the Nile (the sacred river)

Abyssinian, Abora Abyssinia (Ethiopia) is one traditional site of Paradise. Apart from the oriental and paradisal connotations, the maid may be Abyssinian for the pleasing verbal effect of counterpointing 'abyss' with 'mount'. Abora is a second thought; Coleridge first wrote Amora or Amara. Mt Amara is mentioned in Purchas's *Pilgrimage* and occurs in Milton's *Paradise Lost*, Book 4, as a mistakenly conjectured site of Paradise. These names are discussed extensively in J. L. Lowes, *The Road to Xanadu*, Constable, 1927, and in the writings of John Beer

dulcimer an instrument on which sounds are produced, as in the piano, by hammers striking strings. The word 'dulcet' means sweet and soothing

THE RIME OF THE ANCIENT MARINER 1797–8, 1817

How a Ship having passed the Line was driven by Storms to the cold Country towards the South Pole; and how from thence she made her course to the tropical latitudes of the Great Pacific and in what manner the Ancyent Marinere came back to his own Country*

* This headnote prefaced the 1798 version of the poem, which used more archaic language. (It appears in the appendix of *Selected Poetry*). The version discussed in this Note was published in 1817.

PART 1

An old sailor meets three wedding guests and detains one

A Wedding-Guest is mesmerised by the Mariner's strangely urgent tale. A fierce gale has driven the Mariner's ship into Antarctica. An Albatross appears and is welcomed by the crew. It seems to bring good luck, for the ship finds its way safely northwards through ice and fog. Yet the Mariner confesses he shot the Albatross.

Is it important that the encounter takes place on a threshold, and at a wedding, and that hypnotism is implied? Why 'one of three'? Do the stanzas with internal rhymes have a particular purpose? Are all the marginal comments of the same kind? Is the marginal commentator attempting to impose a reading on the poem, and if so why? (Some have argued that these later 'glosses' represent Coleridge's Christian mind attempting to make the poem's world seem less arbitrary in moral terms). If the shooting of the albatross is a 'crime', what 'law' makes it so?

Clearly, like the icicles in 'Frost at Midnight', the fountains in 'Kubla Khan', the moon in *Christabel*, and the harp in several poems, the Albatross is a symbol. By what means does it become so? How many interpretations of the symbol can you find suggested in the text itself? Would you argue for or against suggestions that the Albatross is to be identified with Christ himself, or with Coleridge's own imagination?

Facile credo ... T. Burnet Thomas Burnet (author of the Latin headnote, which Coleridge has modified to suit his own purposes) was a seventeenth-century Neoplatonist

An ancient Mariner stoppeth the marginal notes are in an antique English, designed to project the poem into the past, as if it were a medieval text being pored over by a Renaissance scholar

eftsoons (archaic) soon afterwards

kirk (Scottish) church

PART 2

After the slaying of the Albatross, the ship is becalmed, and the sailors tormented by drought

The ship sails north, still in mist. The sailors protest that it was unwise to kill the bird which brought them a southerly wind, but as the mists clear they change their tune. They enter a 'silent sea' and sail on until they are becalmed at the equator 'upon the slimy sea'. Superstition takes hold of the sailors. Believing that the Mariner has offended one of the spirits, they make him wear the Albatross about his neck, in place of the crucifix.

Why is the ship's change of direction signalled (line 83) in quite this way? The poem and the prose gloss seem to understand the world in different ways. For instance, the marginal comments on lines 87–102 appear anxious to explain that the sailors deserve the fate the poem has in store for them, and to make the geography of the poem more specific. Coleridge spoke in *Biographia Literaria* of 'that willing suspension of disbelief which constitutes poetic faith': does the penultimate comment on Part 2, concerning Michael Psellus, help you to suspend your disbelief?

uprist rose up

Ah! well-a-day! 'what a woeful time it was!'

PART 3

The Nightmare Life-in-Death wins the Mariner's soul; Death wins the crew

The Mariner sees in the distance a skeleton ship, with neither wind nor current to propel her, which drives between them and the setting sun: her only crew are spectres, 'Death' and 'Life-in-Death'. As they arrive the spectres are casting dice. Life-in-Death wins the game, as night falls: her prize is the Mariner's soul. Two hundred sailors die that night, 'And every soul, it passed me by/ Like the whizz of my cross-bow!'

When the 'skeleton-ship' or 'naked hulk' comes between the Mariner and the sun, why does he compare it to a dungeon-grate? And why has the word 'cross' or 'cross-bow' appeared in the last or next last line of each part so far? They seem to connect the Mariner's action with the crucifixion of Christ, but do you feel the poem is set in a Christian world? It seems strange that a Christian poet would present the fate of Christian souls as settled by a game of dice, but Coleridge *may* be expressing a view (or indeed a dread or nightmare) concerning arbitrary salvation or damnation.

unslaked unsatisfied (that is, dry)

hulk the term may imply a prison-ship

Heaven's Mother Mary, mother of Jesus ('Mother of God')

clomb climbed

PART 4

Involuntarily the Mariner blesses the water-snakes

When the Wedding-Guest fears he is listening to a ghost, the Mariner assures him, 'this body dropped not down'. Yet his experience was worse than death. He is alone among slimy and rotting things, unable to avoid the curse he sees in the eyes of his dead companions, unable to die or to pray. In line 263 the moon rises, as if it has never done so before, and beautifies the sky and the sea. In its clear, cool light the Mariner is revived enough to watch the 'water-snakes' and admire their strange beauty. 'A spring of love gushed from my heart ... / And I blessed them unaware.' The 'spring' makes prayer possible, and the Albatross 'fell off and sank/ Like lead into the sea'.

The physical and mental horrors may echo conditions on the slave ships which plied the Atlantic. Of the seven stanzas dealing with a world of death two are marked by different lengths. What effects do these have? If you have observed the role of the moon in other poems by Coleridge you will know that the reference to the moon in line 263 foretells a change. It also provokes the marginal commentator into a sort of parallel prose poem, which some have seen as a cry from Coleridge's heart as he composed it in 1817 (during his own opium agonies). Does it seem, also, to fit into any clear pattern of symbolism? Clearly the moon brings comfort, where the sun torments, yet in Part 2 the 'glorious sun' was described as 'like God's own head'. Is this a consistent symbolic universe? The blessing of the water-snakes is described as being performed 'unaware': can one 'bless' while 'unaware'?

PART 5
A troop of spirits work the vessel, and while the Mariner is in a faint the spirits of the region discuss his fate
Sleep follows prayer, and rain follows sleep, as heaven-sent gifts (here the editor seems to take his interpretation from the Mariner). The Mariner dreams of dew, and wakes to find it raining. An uncanny storm follows in which, through lightning and rain, the moon and stars still shine. Without wind (like the spectre-bark in Part 3) the ship moves on. The dead bodies of his ship-mates rise and 'work the ropes', animated by 'a troop of spirits'. At dawn the bodies emit sweet sounds like a chorus of angels, and the Mariner is cheered by sounds like those of birds and instruments; even the sails sound like a stream in June. The motion of the

ship is caused by supernatural agency, the Polar spirit. In a swoon, the Mariner hears two other spirits discuss his crime.

Why does this section contain the first and only reference to the Mariner having any relations and what effect does it have? Why is the sea journey described in heath and woodland imagery in lines 358–72? If the references to skylarks and hidden brooks suggest that we should value such gifts more, this section is preparing for the poem's conclusion. Lines 398–406 of the poem, in which the words 'cross', 'bow' and 'Albatross' recur, along with 'penance', may imply a Christian reading of the poem, just as the commentary has been insisting.

silly (archaic, from the German selig) blessed

jargoning twittering, but related to 'jargon' meaning unfamiliar or unintelligible speech

PART 6
By supernatural agency the Mariner's ship returns to his home port
The second voice and the marginal gloss explain what causes the vessel's supernatural speed. The Mariner awakes to find himself sailing in fair weather, but still observed by the crew of 'dead men'. As he enters harbour he sees a seraph standing by each corpse. A rowing-boat approaches, bringing the Pilot and his boy, and a Hermit. The sound of the Hermit's voice brings hope to the Mariner: 'He'll shrieve my soul, he'll wash away/ The Albatross's blood'.

Along with the imagery of death (the sailors fitter for 'a charnel-dungeon') images of returning life, springtime and welcoming hint at the Mariner's yearning for normality. Why is the quiet ocean described in line 414 as 'still as a slave before his lord'? Lines 465–8 repeat the images of lines 21–4 in reverse order, except that the return is made by moonlight. The reanimation / deanimation of the dead sailors, like the Mariner's change from prayerlessness to prayerfulness, and his feeling forgiven at some moments yet unforgiven at others, may express Coleridge's own religious anxieties.

shrieve (archaic) to hear a penitent's confession, assign penance and absolve from sin

PART 7

The Mariner's eternal penance begins, alienated from human kind
Those in the pilot's boat discuss the strange appearance of the ship and its now vanished seraph-lights. A thunderous sound is heard, and the ship sinks; the stunned Mariner is pulled aboard the Pilot's boat. When he tries to speak, the Pilot faints, his boy goes crazy, and the Hermit begins to pray – so the Mariner has to row the boat himself. Ashore, confession relieves his agony. But the Mariner's penance cannot end. He goes 'like night, from land to land' and has 'strange power of speech'; and wherever he goes he recognises those who need to hear his tale – men like the Wedding-Guest. The Mariner's last words are a message to him, concerning the loneliness of the soul without God, the necessity of prayer, and the uselessness of prayer without love. The Mariner is gone. Only the Wedding-Guest remains, 'stunned' and 'forlorn'.

The sinking of the ship, the fact that the Mariner is pulled from the sea 'as swift as dreams' and the reactions of the Pilot's boy and the hermit, all emphasise that his experience has belonged to 'another dimension'. Is this dimension in the supernatural realm or in the psyche? The Mariner may have been roaming for centuries as well as from land to land. So who *or what* is he? In Wordworth's poetry such figures arise ambiguously as if sent by Heaven, or emerging 'from some far region' of the soul, as in 'The Leech-Gatherer' and 'The Discharged Soldier', to give 'admonishment': it may be helpful to think of the Mariner in psychological terms as an archetype of the unconscious, one of the basic symbols which recur in dreams and myths, or as a timeless, immortal wanderer gifted with strange wisdom.

How well does the moral expounded in lines 610–17 deal with the questions the narrative has implanted in your mind? Coleridge, when a reader complained that the poem was insufficiently moral, replied that, if anything, its moral was too explicit. How would you assess its moral implications?

Do we ever learn why the Mariner chose the Wedding-Guest? Does his brusqueness and irreverence justify this selection? Perhaps in the terms of the 'Dejection' ode, where wedding imagery is also used, he is one of the 'poor loveless ever-anxious crowd' and needs instruction in the meaning of the words 'love', 'union' and 'prayer'. Perhaps the Mariner is 'sent' to instruct the Wedding-Guest in a 'sacramental' view of life if he is to appreciate the sacrament he has just attended. But if the tale teaches him that there is 'one Life' (a standard reading of the encounter), why does he turn from the bridegroom's door, and what makes him 'sadder' the morrow morn?

Do you find the poem's epigraph from Burnet, implying that the world is full of spiritual agents, comforting or frightening? If there is really *is* a moral universe, might this be a terrifying idea?

CHRISTABEL 1798, 1800
The Tale of Christabel and the enigmatic Geraldine

PART 1
Christabel, while praying for her distant lover, discovers the mysterious Geraldine, who casts a spell over her

LINES 1–70
The scene is a castle, at midnight, marked not only by owls but more uncannily by a crowing cock, and by Sir Leoline's 'mastiff bitch' which 'answers' the cock. In the wood beyond the gate, Christabel is praying for her 'betrothed knight' (like the maid in 'The Nightingale' she is a child of nature), when she is startled by a moan. This comes not from the wind (lines 45–52 specify how still it is) but from 'a damsel bright'.

Curious disturbances mark the narrative. The word order in '… the crowing cock; / Tu-whit! – To-whoo!' deliberately blurs cock and owl (as in Wordsworth's 'The Idiot Boy': 'The cocks did crow tu-whoo, tu-whoo) while the notion of a mastiff bitch marking the quarters and hours with 'sixteen short howls' is even more bizarre. The moon is full yet small. Less obviously, if the moaning (line 39) only 'seems' to come from the other side of the oak, might it come from the oak itself? Given that the narrator exclaims 'Jesu, Maria, shield her well!' in line 54, it is not wholly clear whether Christabel speaks line 69 or only line 70. Interpretations based on these matters are discussed in Part Three.

LINES 71–189

To explain her presence, Geraldine claims that she has been kidnapped by warriors, brought far on horseback, and left beneath the oak. Christabel offers the hospitality of her father's house, and they enter the sleeping castle. Geraldine has to be carried across the threshold, and as they pass, the mastiff bitch moans ominously in her sleep. The embers of the fire in the hall react with 'a fit of flame' as the women pass silently to Christabel's bedroom.

> Do we share Christabel's faith in the 'stout chivalry' of Sir Leoline's household? Why are we told that 'an army in battle array had marched out' through his gates? And is the ill-health of Sir Leoline the only reason Christabel fears to wake him? Why is Christabel's lamp as 'dead and dim' as the moon? These **Gothic** touches may be tongue-in-cheek, or may hint at an oppressive environment: one may wonder whose warriors have molested Geraldine, and whether all is well with father–daughter relations in Langdale Hall.

LINES 190–234

To revive her guest, Christabel offers a glass of healing cordial. This was made by her mother, who died in childbirth, saying that she would, though dead, hear Christabel's wedding-bells. Geraldine reacts strangely, staring as if at the ghost of Christabel's mother, and warning her that 'this hour is mine'. Christabel soothes Geraldine, who drinks the cordial. Her eyes become bright and she is seen in her full beauty.

> Ambiguities multiply. Who are those who 'live in the upper sky' and why, if Geraldine is allied with those who love Christabel, is she jealous of her mother?

LINES 235–78

Geraldine speaks courteously, blessing Christabel and telling her to prepare for bed. But Christabel watches Geraldine carefully, and sees 'her bosom and half her side – / A sight to dream of, not to tell', at which the narrator exclaims, 'O shield her! shield sweet Christabel'. Geraldine takes

Christabel in her arms and warns her that the touch of her breast will cast a spell over the girl, sealing her lips.

In revising the poem Coleridge removed a line explaining that Geraldine's breast and side appear withered and 'foul of hue', creating considerable ambiguity as to whether Christabel is threatened with seduction or witchcraft, and what it is that Christabel will not be able (or willing) to 'tell'. But he left the reference (in line 270) to 'this mark of my shame'. What kind of struggle is taking place in Geraldine in lines 257–61? Is there an implication that she is there to carry out a task she feels guilty about?

LINES 279–331

The conclusion to Part 1 reverts to the oak tree and the lovely sight of Christabel at her prayers, contrasting her beauty and tranquillity then with her anxiety now; but 'the worker of these harms' sleeps peacefully. The 'hour' of Geraldine's power has passed. While it lasted even the owls were silent; now they call again. Christabel, too, relaxes. Though crying, she also smiles, as though her mother's guardian spirit were near.

What do you suppose took place in the hour of Geraldine's power? Is Christabel in bliss or pain? How much grasp does the narrator appear to have of his story? The question and doubts in lines 322–28 contrast uncertainly with the pious hope of lines 329–31.

mastiff a large, strong dog, frequently found in Romances or horror stories because of its frightening appearance, somewhat muted in this instance by her toothlessness

up this way the setting of the poem is unclear in Part 1 (written in Somerset) but is specified in Part 2 as the Lake District of north-west England

mistletoe a plant mentioned in various legends and myths, supposedly sacred to the Druids (the ancient Celtic priesthood)

PART 2
Geraldine casts a different kind of spell over Sir Leoline, Christabel's father, blinding him to the warnings of Bard Bracy who has dreamt of a threat to Christabel

LINES 332–92
It is morning, marked as always in Sir Leoline's castle by the tolling of a bell in memory of his wife. The sounds re-echo, and according to the bard are answered by distant bells rung by the ghosts of 'sextons' and by the devil himself, from various places in the Lake District. Geraldine wakes, shakes off 'her dread' (is she more suffering than evil?) and wakens Christabel – who is still perplexed, as by a dream, but is struck by Geraldine's gentleness and beauty.

Does Christabel grasp in lines 370–3 that Geraldine is a dual being? Do lines 379–80 imply physical duality also? And why does Christabel say 'Sure I have sinned'?

LINES 394–446
The Baron warmly welcomes his guest. He and Geraldine's father – Lord Roland de Vaux of Tryermaine (whose melodious name he murmurs to himself) – were firm friends in youth. Their friendship has been turned to enmity through gossip, but neither has found as good a friend again, or could wholly forget the other. Sir Leoline remembers the youthful Lord Roland, and vows to find and punish those who have harmed his friend's daughter, whom he embraces fondly.

Lines 408–26 were admired by nineteenth-century readers as the most 'wholesome' element in the poem: perhaps this depiction of manly friendship came as a relief from the ambiguities of the Christabel/Geraldine, Leoline/Christabel, Leoline/Geraldine liaisons.

LINES 447–518
Watching this embrace, prolonged by Geraldine, Christabel is reminded of what she saw the previous night. In her shock she 'hisses' so sharply that the knight looks round – but Christabel is smiling again under

Geraldine's spell. She cannot tell what is wrong, when her father asks. Geraldine tactfully offers to leave at once. Sir Leoline will not hear of it. He decides to send Bard Bracy to Lord Roland's home on the Scottish border with a message that his daughter is safe and that his old friend longs to see him.

What does Christabel see in the embrace of Geraldine and her father? And what is the source of the 'rapture' which succeeds her vision of fear?

LINES 519–63

Bracy, however, asks for a delay. He has had a dream, or a vision, of threatening evil: a dove was attacked by a bright green snake 'coiled around its wings and neck'. The snake was 'couched' with the dove in the same vaguely erotic, yet threatening way as that in which Geraldine was sharing Christabel's couch.

There is a momentary ambiguity in lines 548–9, 'I stooped, methought, the dove to take / When lo! I saw a bright green snake' before we reach the next line, 'Coiled around its wings and neck'. Is it possible to dispel the slight uncertainty created here?

LINES 564–620

To the Baron, though, the dove represents Geraldine, and the snake her enemies, whom he promises to crush. He kisses Geraldine, who glances at Christabel with eyes shrunken and dull like a serpent's. Again Christabel shudders 'with a hissing sound' and while Geraldine turns her 'large bright eyes divine' on the father, the daughter can only stare at them. Under Geraldine's influence, Christabel's eyes imitate 'that look of dull and treacherous hate', as far as is possible, that is, with 'eyes so innocent and blue'. Recovering from her trance, she begs her father to send 'this woman away', but can give no reason.

What is the significance of the moment when Geraldine 'couched her head upon her breast' (line 580): is she mocking the bard? And who sees her eyes as divine (line 595), the narrator, Sir Leoline or the poet? Lines 583–620 appear to dramatise the possession of Christabel by Geraldine. How are these lines prepared for in the earlier symbolism of the poem? Is there any clear signal that this possession is evil?

LINES 621–55

Sir Leoline, under the spell of Geraldine's beauty, forgets his love for his daughter and feels only rage that she should dishonour him by such rudeness. Abruptly he orders Bracy to depart. Ignoring his daughter, Sir Leoline leaves with Geraldine.

As the narrative ends here one would expect these last lines to be especially significant in an interpretation of the poem. If the poem is unfinished, this may not be the case. Do you find them helpful in arriving at a reading?

LINES 656–77

The little child, 'a limber elf', referred to here is no longer Christabel but Coleridge's own child Hartley.

Why is the poem unfinished? Is it that any resolution would be an anti-climax? Or that the theme was becoming too overtly sexual for Coleridge to pursue? The closing lines are (like those at the end of 'The Nightingale') 'a father's tale'. They can be read as an excuse for Sir Leoline, suggesting that his anger is a result of excess of love, and that he is dallying with 'wrong that does no harm'. But Geoffrey Yarlott has argued (in *Coleridge and the Abyssinian Maid*) that in these lines Coleridge recognises that his troubling fiction applies all too closely to his own domestic situation: in love with an intruder (Sara Hutchinson) and resentful of his children.

In 1825 Coleridge recalled: 'Even in boyhood there was a cold hollow spot, an aching in the heart, when I said my prayers – that prevented my entire union with God – that I could not give up, or that would not give me up – *as if a snake had wreathed around my heart, & at this one spot its mouth touched at & inbreathed a weak incapability of willing it away*'. One of the surprising things about Coleridge is that his apparently objective narratives are as personal as the confessional poems – sometimes more so. In this case, Coleridge's own paralysis of the will and boyhood difficulties in prayer seem to have symbolised themselves in Christabel's trance, and perhaps her seduction.

Geraldine, whether good or ill, victim or victimiser, or victim become victimiser, is a powerfully ambiguous recreation of the *femme fatale*. She can be compared to Keats's fairy-tale figure in 'La belle dame sans merci' and his 'Lamia' of whom it is never entirely clear, nor meant to be, whether she is a serpent in disguise or woman in love. Are Coleridge and Keats examining or simply expressing male fear of the female?

sacristan (archaic) sexton (line 353)

Five and forty beads must tell a reference to 'counting' prayer-beads, each bead standing for a particular prayer. Coleridge's medieval poems use such references to Roman Catholic practices for atmospheric effect. The appeal to 'Jesu, Maria' in line 54 is another example

vests ... breasts the line implies that Christabel is confused by the appearance of 'heaving breasts' where, the previous night, Geraldine's breasts were withered

presence room the room where the Baron receives guests

tourney court field for armed contests between individual knights

bosom old ... bosom cold these lines make explicit the implied content of lines 252–3 and explain Christabel's returning warmth in lines 324–5

bard poet or minstrel (in a sense Bracy is Coleridge's poetic representative in this poem, and in some readings the person most likely to intuit the real nature of Geraldine)

heaves ... swelling this part of the dream refers to the courting display of doves and snakes, and has further erotic significance

resigned to controlled by

limber lithe, nimble

LOVE 1799

The poet tells us a story of the happy consequences of telling his beloved Genevieve the doleful ballad of a knight whose love was returned only as he lay dying

In a romantic setting, with his beloved Genevieve leaning against the statue of an armed knight, the poet indulges himself in a sad tale of such a knight, while watching the effects of his tale on the blushing listener. In the tale the knight has been scorned by his lady, until his wits are crazed; he eventually rescues 'the Lady of the Land' from a fate worse than death; she nurses him in a cave until, as he lay dying, his madness went away. The effect of the tale, however, is that Genevieve is reduced to tears, embraces the narrator, and marries him.

In Coleridge's lifetime 'Love' was, with *The Ancient Mariner,* his most admired poem. It moves artfully from the Romantic idealism of the opening stanza to the heady eroticism of the close, which is in fact prefigured in the body-language of the poet lying 'midway on the mount' and Genevieve leaning 'against the armed man'. Both attitudes seem coyly expressive of what Milton (in *Paradise Lost*) called Eve's 'sweet reluctant amorous delay'. The characters and events are doubled; the wooing poet and the knight, the Lady of the Land and Genevieve mingle as do the moonlight and the lights of eve. The ballad lady's scorn of the knight's tragic love is matched by Genevieve's downcast eyes at the start; her recognition of him permits Genevieve to gaze on the narrator's face at the close, and as the ballad lady nurses her knight, so Geraldine embraces the balladeer.

At an obvious level the poet figures as seducer, yet desire is mutual and the 'music' of the ballad releases other 'gentle wishes long subdued'. Genevieve's innocence is constantly stressed, yet at the close her embrace is in part 'a bashful art, / That I might rather feel, than see, / The swelling of her heart'.

The poem is heady and sensuous. Is it also rather alarming? Clearly the Lady of the Land is another forerunner of Keats's 'La belle dame sans merci', and there is a sense of fatalism beneath the apparent idealism in the opening declaration that 'All thoughts, all passions, all delights … All are but ministers of Love / And feed his sacred flame'. Perhaps the most striking parallel is that between the cruelty of the Lady of the Land (who has crazed the knight before she nurses him) and the narrator whose entire performance can be seen as a calculated gambit of seduction, aimed at creating the fears he calms.

DEJECTION: AN ODE   APRIL 1802

Listening dejectedly to the moans of an Aeolian harp the poet is convinced that he has lost the shaping power of imagination; now he can only listen to the creativity of others, and pray that his friends will always know the joy he can never regain

In the first of the eight strophes of the ode, the poet depicts his favourite images of wind and moon. The state of the moon reminds him of an ancient ballad in which stormy weather is foretold from such a phenomenon. As yet his Aeolian harp is only sobbing dully: the sound irritates him and appears to express his own dull feelings. The sobbing lute and the phantom radiance of the moon combine the images now familiar to us from the conversation poems. But here he is not soothed by them: he longs for the promised storm to come, so that he may feel awed and elevated, startled into similar agitation.

The second strophe specifies his unimpassioned mood in terms of void and dreariness. Though 'wooed' by the thrush, he has gazed blankly on the beautiful appearances of sky and clouds and stars. They only increase his despair: 'I see, not feel how beautiful they are!'

The third section reflects on this state of mind. If his own 'genial spirits' fail, what can mere appearances do to cheer him? He could watch for ever, but the outer light will not help unless he also has within himself 'passion and life'. The same thought is presented more philosophically in the fourth section, where he refutes the idea that the mind can be elevated by outward things. Nature 'lives' only because man bestows beauty, life and meaning upon it. The transforming light of the moon is only an image for the beautifying light that the 'soul' sheds on what it loves. (We feel that moonlight is beautiful only if we are spiritual enough to see the moonlight's likeness to spirit.)

For the activity of the creative soul Coleridge uses the terms 'light', 'luminous mist' and 'music', all suggesting its 'beauty-making power'. But in the fifth strophe he chooses one term – Joy. In the Romantic period Joy was used to denote a state of being in which there is such internal harmony of spirit that it overflows from the pure soul to beautify the world around. In a state of joy we are 'wedded' to nature (line 68), and the 'dowry' of this wedding is 'a new Earth and a new Heaven'. Whatever charms us – all colours or melodies, appealing to eye or ear (line 73) – is a reflection of our own joy.

In the sixth strophe Coleridge looks back on his life, seeing the waning of this joy. In the past his inner joy made him able to 'dally' with distress. Sustained by hope, he felt he was creative. Now (line 81) he wonders whether he was in fact sustained by the inner strength of others, for now he has no inner resources to meet his afflictions. In lines 87–93 he appears to regret his investigative analytical pursuits: perhaps the scientific detachment of 'abstruse research' has so infected his whole being that he is now incapable of spontaneous joy.

The seventh strophe brings a change of mood. Coleridge shakes off his 'viperous' thoughts. The lute has ceased to moan. The wind is raving, and the scream of the lute makes Coleridge think of the mountain landscape all around – which is a 'fitter' instrument for such a wind. From the passive lute Coleridge turns his attention to the wind, which he likens to an actor or a poet, expert in tragic art. In the wind he hears a tale of warriors in defeat; and then a more tender song of a lost and frightened child.

From thoughts of the wider world, its tragedies, and the creative powers at work in it, Coleridge returns to addressing the 'Lady' of strophes 2, 4 and 5. The end of the poem is a prayer that she might be watched over by the bright stars; and that she – unlike the poet – may be visited by healing sleep, and attuned to joy.

In 'The Eolian Harp' the poet compared himself to the harp, and his thoughts to its music. How differently is the harp symbol used here?

Has he also changed his view of Nature? Is nature 'dead'? Can you reconcile the picture of nature in this poem with the 'one Life' in the earlier poems? If he has lost his spirit of Imagination, how is this shown in the opening stanzas?

This is a second great defeat. Having disowned the revolutionary ardour of his youth he has now lost, also, the capacity for inner happiness which took its place. If so was it ever really his? Did it have any reality? Were his beliefs in the life of nature and

the creative imagination just illusions? Was 'Frost at Midnight'
true?

yestreen last evening
Sir Patrick Spence one of the best-known ballads in Bishop Percy's *Reliques
of Ancient English Poetry* (1765)
O Lady! the lady is Sara Hutchinson (see also 'A Letter to —' below). The
concluding prayer of the poem is a gift to her, as the woman he loves most
deeply. But the argument of this version of the poem is really addressed to
Wordsworth. The first published version of the poem (in *The Morning Post*,
4 October 1802, Wordsworth's wedding day) has 'O Edmund'. A version
transcribed in a letter to Southey, 19 July 1802, is explicitly addressed to
Wordsworth
give away their motion that is, they make the stars appear to move
genial in Coleridge's day the primary meaning of the word was 'generative',
'connected with creative genius'. The 'generative' meaning is associated
also with wedded love, so the phrase is linked with (a) Coleridge's marital
unhappiness, (b) the 'wedding' imagery of lines 49 and 68
forms shapes or 'things'. Philosophically, 'outward forms' implies material
entities as opposed to the realm of eternal ideas
fountains a key image in many poems, associated with 'springs' of
creativity
we receive but what we give Wordsworth believed in the interaction of nature
and the mind, so Coleridge appears to be questioning one of Wordsworth's
most characteristic beliefs
wedding-garment ... shroud one of the basic themes of Romanticism was
that materialist philosophy changed the living world into a world of death.
Coleridge is not identifying himself with materialist thought, but he is
lamenting that if the observer is not full of joy the world is, subjectively,
dead to him
Joy the reiteration of joy here is similar to that in a famous German
Romantic poem Friedrich Schiller's 'Ode to Joy'. Schiller's text is sung by
the chorus in Beethoven's Ninth Symphony with its triumphant repetition of
'Freude ... Freude' ('Joy ... Joy')
We in ourselves rejoice! Wordsworth testifies in his poetry that if one looks
into the 'life of things' one finds that joy is the basis of all life. Coleridge
appears to retort here that the joy we find in nature is really in ourselves

There was a time an allusion to the first line of Wordsworth's ode, 'Intimations of Immortality': 'There was a time when meadow, grove, and stream / ... To me did seem / Apparelled in celestial light'
Otway's self Thomas Otway (1652–85), a dramatic poet. Line 210 of the verse letter refers rather more pertinently to 'William's self' as the author of the 'tender lay' (Wordsworth's 'Lucy Gray' comes to mind). But Otway, who died a tragic early death, was for Coleridge one of those whose lives embody the fatality of being a poet, others being Chatterton, the subject of Coleridge's 'Monody on the death of Chatterton' (1790–4).

A LETTER TO — [SARAH HUTCHINSON] 1802

Note: Though the text of the Oxford World's Classics 'Letter' (see Appendix), based on a manuscript copied by Mary Wordworth, is in numbered sections or strophes, giving it an appearance of similar formality to the ode, in the Everyman version, based on a different manuscript, the poem is simply paragraphed, making it look closer in style to the 'conversation poems'.

LINES 1–43 (SECTIONS 1–3)
The letter begins with a paragraph almost identical to the first **strophe** of the **ode**, except that Sara is addressed in line 15. The account of dread is the same, except that Coleridge appeals to Sara as one who knows what he suffers. The singing thrush (lines 24–9) is more specifically located in a larch tree coming into leaf. By placing the words 'vainly wooed' (which refer to the thrush's song) next to 'O dearest Sara', Coleridge delicately alludes to his love for her. The moon of lines 39–40 is also made more personal: his image of the moon becalmed in its blue lake is now associated with 'dear William's sky canoe' (a reference to Wordsworth's poem 'Peter Bell').

LINES 44–183 (SECTIONS 4–13)
Lines 44–51 correspond to lines 39–46 of the ode, but lines 52–183 appear in the letter alone. The 'green light' **image** (line 49) now introduces the thought that Sara may be watching the same light. Even this thought moves him only feebly, although he remembers that as a schoolboy he was moved to ecstatic yearnings by such sights and

reflections. Yet in lines 74–98 it appears that his despair at non-feeling was rash, for the reflection has affected him: he imagines Sara in two favourite places (a weather-fended wood, and a sod-built seat of Camomile) and he is, after all, moved by the thought. Imagining her, he sees in her eyes a 'prayer' meant for him: his response is to bless her.

Lines 99–110 recall an evening with Mary and Sara, when he enjoyed the innocent affection of both sisters. Such remembrances of joy revive him; but he wonders why he was unable to recall such memories a short time before. Line 115 refers to having written a complaining letter to Sara. Perhaps overdramatically, he blames Sara's present sickness (lines 116–29) on this letter. The letter seems to have concerned the feelings between them (or the lack of them on her part) for in lines 130–78 he makes an attempt to persuade her that he will not claim more than she can give. Her well-being and tranquillity are all he desires, and he will be content to think of William, Mary, Dorothy and Sara living together in happiness. Yet he would rather not see their happiness, as temporary visits only increase his pain. The imagery of lines 160–8 makes plain the strength of Coleridge's feeling that he is an outsider, unable to share fully in their joy: he feels himself to be 'A wither'd branch upon a blossoming Tree'. He will be content to share her delights at a distance, but he confesses that he cannot bear to be unable to comfort her when she is in need.

LINES 184–247 (SECTIONS 14–16)
We return to the sound of the lute and the now raving wind (as in lines 94–133 of the ode). The prayer that his friend may enjoy gentle and healing sleep is followed in this poem by another personal lament over his own lack of buoyancy, but that lack is explained differently. Now the complaint is more pointed: 'E'er I was wedded, though my path was rough' (lines 231). A further reference to Coleridge's domestic discord – 'two unequal minds / ... and two discordant wills' – adds to the sense of grievance (lines 242–7).

LINES 248–94 (SECTIONS 17–18)
The poet develops a contrast here between Wordsworth's family of love and his own 'coarse' domestic life. His 'abstruse research' appears, in this context, to have been a way of trying to distract himself from this sense

of grievance, though this claim is not entirely convincing in the light of Coleridge's biography. Even the joy he finds in his own children reminds him of how much he has lost; at times he feels resentment at being burdened by them, and cramped in his intellectual flights (line 279). In section 19 even the scenes of the Lake District 'are not to me now the / 'Things which once they were'. The letter ends with passages equivalent to strophes 4 and 5 of the ode, and a modified version of its final lines.

The relation between the two 'dejection' poems of 1802 is controversial. Most critics assume that 'Dejection: An Ode' is a revision of 'A Letter to — [Sara Hutchinson]'. George Dekker's powerful arguments against this view are discussed in Part 3. The 'Letter' includes the entire text of the ode, though the sections are rearranged.

There are several obvious questions about this poem, in relation to 'Dejection: An Ode'. Does it offer the same explanation for Coleridge's dejection? If not, which explanation is true? Might both of them be true? Which argument is easier to follow? Which poem is more revealing? Does that make it truer? What do you make of the fact that various versions exist, addressed to 'O Lady', 'Sara', and 'Edmund'?

You might go through this poem sidelining the lines which occur in the ode. Having done that, you might ask yourself whether the lines which only occur in the 'Letter' are as good, *as poetry*, as those which occur in both. Which is likelier: that he wrote the ode and then added lines to make a personal version of it addressed to Sara, or that he wrote the 'Letter' and then cut out the personal revelations to leave himself with the ode?

O Sister! Sara's sister Mary was about to become Wordsworth's wife, and of course Dorothy's sister-in-law. All four of them looked on Coleridge as a brother

I too will crown me with a Coronal an allusion to Wordsworth's 'Immortality Ode', line 40 ('My head hath its coronal').

PART THREE

CRITICAL APPROACHES

ROMANTIC IMAGINATION

COLERIDGE'S DEFINITIONS

In Chapter 4 of *Biographia Literaria* (1817), Coleridge recollects hearing Wordsworth read his poem 'The Female Vagrant'. What struck him, he says, was:

> the union of deep feeling with profound thought; the fine balance of truth in observing with the imaginative faculty in modifying the objects observed; and above all the original gift of spreading the tone, the *atmosphere*, and with it the depth and height of the ideal world, around forms, incidents, and situations of which, for the common view, custom had bedimmed all the lustre, had dried up the sparkle and the dew drops.

Repeated meditation led him to suspect that 'fancy and imagination were two distinct and widely different faculties', rather than two words for the same thing. In Chapter 13 he returned to these 'widely different faculties' and offered the following definitions:

> The IMAGINATION, then, I consider either as primary, or secondary. The primary Imagination I hold to be the living power and prime agent of all human perception, and as a repetition in the finite mind of the eternal act of creation in the infinite I AM. The secondary I consider as an echo of the former, coexisting with the conscious will, yet still as identical with the primary in the *kind* of its agency, and differing only in *degree*, and in the mode of its operation. It dissolves, diffuses, dissipates, in order to recreate; or where this process is rendered impossible, yet still, at all events, it struggles to idealise and to unify. It is essentially *vital*, even as all objects (*as* objects) are essentially fixed and dead.

> FANCY, on the contrary, has no other counters to play with but fixities and definites. The fancy is indeed no other than a mode of memory emancipated from the order of time and space; and blended with, and modified by that empirical phenomenon of the will which we express by the word CHOICE. But equally with the ordinary memory it must receive all its materials ready made from the law of association.

These famous definitions are, unfortunately, among the least immediately intelligible of the statements about **Imagination** in the Romantic period, and it is only when Coleridge speaks of imagination as 'the distinguishing characteristic of man as a progressive being' (in his 'Essay on Education') that he really touches on the centrality of Imagination to the Romantic view of human life. In this broader sense, also, he speaks in his early political lectures of Robespierre as a man of Imagination – someone capable of conceiving human life as it might be rather than as it is.

For some eighteenth-century minds, Imagination was a disease from which poets were prone to suffer: something very close to fantasy. For others it was simply the faculty of forming **images**: the more imaginative you were, the more distinctly you could remember or draw something that was not present to you. The Romantics jettisoned both of these contradictory ideas – the idea of imagination as a synonym for either memory or fantasy. They made it the central mental power – basic to all perception, intuition, speculative thought, love, friendship, and of course creativity.

For William Blake the 'Poetic Genius', which is in all of us, is 'the true man'. Without our poetic genius we would be condemned to repeating the same ideas endlessly, and incapable of progression. Wordsworth defines Imagination in Book 14 of *The Prelude* as 'clearest insight, amplitude of mind, / and Reason in her most exalted mood'. Elsewhere, in a rather uncharacteristic utterance, which is close to Coleridge's Platonic position, Wordsworth says (according to Henry Crabb Robinson's Diary for 11 September 1816) that 'imagination is the faculty by which the poet conceives and produces – that is, *images* [as a verb] – individual forms in which are embodied universal ideas or abstractions.' Percy Bysshe Shelley, in speaking of Imagination in his 'Defence of Poetry', gives an immensely eloquent account of imagination in its moral dimension. For him, because imagination enables the individual to put himself in the place of others, making their own pleasures and pains his own, Imagination is 'the great instrument of moral good'. Keats went even further, claiming in a letter of 1817 that 'What the imagination seizes as beauty must be truth – whether it existed before or not'. If the imagination tells you that we live in a living universe, we do: even if it takes environmental sciences another 150 years to explain what that means.

REASON & UNDERSTANDING

Coleridge's own thinking about Imagination is not really separable from his key distinction between **Reason** and Understanding, a distinction he derived ultimately from Plato and Immanuel Kant (see Philosophical Background). Reason is 'pure and impersonal', unaffected by our selfish passions or by natural or acquired habits of understanding. Coleridge describes it as the latent presence of God in us, yet as 'something in which we are, not which is in us'. It is an inward beholding of spiritual realities which we apprehend directly, just as our senses apprehend material things. It is 'the organ of the supersensuous', just as the eye is the organ of light. It sees the 'whole' rather than individual phenomena, and deals with ultimate ends. It is possible for a truth to be amenable to Reason, but unamenable to Understanding: or rather for us to mislead ourselves if we seek to reach by the Understanding the kind of truth that only reason can give us. Coleridge said in *Aids to Reflection*:

> Reason is indeed far nearer to SENSE than to Understanding: for Reason is a direct aspect of TRUTH, an inward beholding, having a similar relation to the Intelligible or Spiritual as SENSE has to the Material or Phenomenal ... it is the source and substance of truths above sense.

Understanding is 'the science of phenomena' and gives us merely 'abstract knowledge' of things, as opposed to a substantial sense of the 'one Life' of which we are a part. The Understanding classifies, analyses, measures and relies on our separation as subjects from the objects we observe. When man attempts to use 'the forms and mechanisms of his mere reflective faculty' to probe into spiritual truths (the error of the Empiricist tradition) he is attempting to measure nature and divinity with inadequate tools. For if ultimate mysteries are 'cut and squared for the comprehension of the understanding' the result is 'a universe of death'. Man ends in scepticism and irreligion.

There is a clear implication in Coleridge's work that Reason corresponds to Imagination, and Understanding to Fancy. Understanding and Fancy are empirical faculties, dealing in ready-made phenomena, while Reason and Imagination grasp the 'real' in the Platonic sense – the underlying Ideas of which our world is a shadowy set of Appearances. Wordsworth tends to use Reason and Imagination almost inter-changeably and it is fairly clear that Blake and Keats also mean Reason when they say Imagination, and Understanding when they say Reason. Coleridge, being more of a philosopher, steers clear of this confusion.

PRIMARY & SECONDARY IMAGINATION

Returning to Coleridge's definitions of Imagination, one can see that several major claims are being made for Imagination. First that poetic Imagination – as exercised by a great poet – allows us to reperceive things which our senses have ceased to 'see', and see them as alive and meaningful, with the dew of creation still on them. It defamiliarises them. Secondly, that all human perception is in itself creative: our minds constitute what they see. Your eyes see a flat brown rectangle on two or three legs; touch tells you that it is hard but not metallic; your **primary imagination** provides the third and fourth, hidden legs, and constitutes from all this information a table. Thirdly, that **secondary imagination** is directly analogous to God's creation in that it makes new things out of chaos.

Basically, primary imagination is the capacity to form mental images of what exists whether present or not, and secondary imagination is the capacity to imagine what does not exist. Critics disagree, however, whether primary imagination also sees *into* and *behind* the things it sees. This is partly because primary imagination is a definition of 'perception' and *perception is itself ambiguous*: when you say Jane is a perceptive child you don't mean simply that she can see a blue crayon as a blue crayon. One can argue that primary imagination is more important than secondary imagination because without it we could not live at all. But one can also argue that primary imagination only *copies* God's creation (unless we are deranged) whereas secondary imagination *imitates* God's creative act.

There are three reasons why Coleridge uses such impressive language in talking about primary imagination as 'a repetition in the finite mind of the eternal act of creation in the infinite I AM'. First, it is a mark of the importance Coleridge attached to overthrowing the idea that the mind was passive in any of its perceptive activity ('any system based upon the passivity of mind must be false' said Coleridge, and Kant also insisted that imagination was a necessary ingredient in *all* perception).

Second, by the date of *Biographia* Coleridge was no longer very sympathetic to the idea that man and nature are one: he now attached great
importance to the idea that perception is not merely an outgrowth of
nature, but something which connects human beings to God. Third,
because God did not, in Coleridge's system, create the world then leave
it to its own devices: what exists *only continues to exist because God continu-
ally wills it*, and when we see an object in creation we are, therefore,
reflecting or 'repeating' in our finite minds His eternal creative activity.

The term Imagination is philosophical rather than simply literary,
and it becomes useful in criticism only as a result of the final section of
Coleridge's definition, which desynonymises Imagination from another
poetic faculty, the **Fancy**. All that the Fancy does, according to this
definition, is rearrange ready-made images. This is a creative act in itself,
but of lower worth. Most verse may be the product of the Fancy, but true
poetry requires Imagination. Consider this **simile**: 'And, like a lobster
boiled, the morn / From black to red began to turn'. As Basil Willey
points out (*Nineteenth Century Studies*, 1949) the association between
lobsters and the morning sky is vivid and amusing – but it is merely a
juxtaposition of the Fancy, in which neither image is modified by the
lines. Imagination can make itself felt in the resonance of a single word.
Wordsworth's favourite example was his own line: 'Over his own sweet
voice the Stock-dove broods'. 'Broods' is a one-word **metaphor**. It
combines, Wordsworth himself said, 'the manner in which the bird
reiterates and prolongs her soft notes, as if herself delighting to listen to
it', with the idea of 'a still and quiet satisfaction, like that which may be
supposed inseparable from the continuous process of incubation'. But 'to
brood', your dictionary will tell you, also means to meditate. So
Wordsworth's use of the term simultaneously describes the sounds of the
dove in their rounded perfection, the warmth and softness of the bird
herself, and makes the whole incubation image a metaphor for the poet's
own meditation.

MAJOR THEMES

Coleridge's poetry falls into many poetic genres, yet the themes explored
in his poems are invariably intertwined: whatever their occasion they are

likely to involve his meditations on such matters as God, Nature, and God in nature, human liberty, free will and the creative imagination. Bound up with these are the intense revelations of a remarkable personality: his vivid dreams and nightmares, and his experience of love and friendship, joy and dejection, dread and sin. The themes covered in the poems summarised in Part Two include friendship and brotherhood, every kind of love (sexual, parental and divine), the 'one Life within us and abroad', Nature, Imagination, dejection and joy, prayer, prayerfulness and prayerlessness, retirement and tranquillity, oppression and revolution, apocalypse, the millennium and paradise, childhood, the unconscious – as it reveals itself in dream, reverie, and nightmare – sin and crime, purgatory and redemption.

RELIGION

Coleridge was, at all stages of his career, profoundly religious, and because he was also speculative, he was interested in every variety of religious experience and every stage of human mythology. The keynote of his intellectual career was to arrive at a marriage of **Platonism** and Christian thought, and to show that Christianity was not merely desirable but philosophically true. Coleridge's religion was not merely one of the head, though it did have to satisfy his very keen intellect. He argued himself out of a **Unitarian** position into a Trinitarian one over the course of several years and became a staunch defender of the orthodox Christian concept of God as containing three persons: the Father (man's creator), the Son (man's redeemer) and the Holy Spirit (man's comforter). He did so because a personal God was necessary to him – a God, that is, whom one can address as 'Thou'. A number of modern theologians (most notably the Jewish philosopher Martin Buber) assume that one of the fundamentals of human life is the possibility of an 'I–Thou' relationship between man and man, man and God, man and nature. Coleridge is one of the great interpreters of this idea, which he developed alongside his deepening belief in the Trinity. To Coleridge, the Trinity of God is essential because God, in order to be a personal God, must be able to say 'Thou' – or he would not be an 'I'. 'There can be no I [logically speaking] without a Thou', he wrote. Since this is a philosophical idea, a law, it must be as true of God as it is of man.

Coleridge's religion, then, is profoundly philosophical. But that does not make it abstract. It arises from a deep human need – a conviction that without God he is nothing. Either he is upheld by God, or there is only nothingness. As a Romantic poet, especially in and around 1798, he was attracted to Spinoza's **Pantheism**, a system of belief in which God, man and nature share one substance, or as Coleridge termed it, 'one life'. Yet Pantheism was intellectually unacceptable to Coleridge (a) because by confusing nature and God it did away with the possibility of a personal Creator, and (b) because if God impels all thought, there is no personal freedom.

NATURE & 'THE ONE LIFE'

One of the primary marks of a Romantic artist is an interest in nature. Eighteenth-century thought had led to an artificial distinction between man and nature – between the thinking mind and the dead material world which was the object of its thought. To the Romantics this stress on analytical thought was reductive: they were interested in the vitality of the 'whole man', one of whose essential capacities is that of enjoying a creative relationship with the natural world. The rationalist view was, to them, unrealistic: in separating man from nature it failed to recognise whole areas of human nature. When, says Coleridge, a man's aim is commercial or materialist, he exploits the world as a realm of objects. But when his aim is 'the nurture and evolution of humanity', he seeks what is 'common to the world and to man'. Man cannot understand either himself or nature until he learns 'to comprehend nature in himself'. Romantic poetry, especially as characterised by such critics as M. H. Abrams, used to be summarised as a poetry which aimed to overcome the division between man and organic nature.

In the conversation poems, especially in 'This Lime-Tree Bower My Prison' and 'Frost at Midnight', Coleridge gives the classic expression to this Romantic theme. Underlying them is Coleridge's Christian and **Neoplatonist** version of Wordsworth's love of nature. It is Coleridge's permanent belief that Nature is 'the eternal language which ... God utters', that the physical world is a set of symbols of the unseen world, that the physical world is harmonious, that there is a secret correspondence between the rhythms of nature and the vibrations of the soul (the wave structure of light and sound are analogous to 'this strong music in the soul'). He believed also that as the human imagination is a reflection of God's creative energy, the healthy imaginative mind has a direct apprehension of the divine joy which permeates creation. In 1798, at least, he believed with William and Dorothy Wordsworth that Nature is in some sense conscious and benevolent, and that nature exercises a 'ministry' to the human spirit, reaching out to, educating and healing the soul. The nature he shared with Wordsworth was one in which, as Wordsworth put it, 'every flower enjoys the air it breathes'. Divine, human, natural, animate and apparently inanimate all partake of one substance and are connected in a circuit – the 'one Life within us and abroad' of which the natural condition is Joy. It is in this context that the most commonly accepted reading of *The Ancient Mariner* is that it transposes the Christian drama of sin, purgatory and redemption into a crime against the 'one Life'.

POLITICS

When Coleridge announces in 'Religious Musings' that 'The Lamb of God hath opened the fifth seal' he is participating in a widespread political optimism, shared by most of Coleridge's intellectual circle, and especially by radical dissenters, that an era of universal peace and brotherhood was about to begin.

Increasingly, however, the poets who welcomed the Fall of the Bastille, found themselves having to distinguish between revolutionary ideals and revolutionary practice. The 'September Massacres' of 1792, the execution of the King, the 'Reign of Terror' under Robespierre in 1794 under which thousands were guillotined – and the ruling Directory's acts of war against the Netherlands and the Rhineland – were a chain of events which dismayed English radicals. Nevertheless, when war was declared between England and France in February 1793, Wordsworth, Coleridge and their friends were still essentially in sympathy with France. Both had friends who were imprisoned in 1794 on charges of treason (for inflammatory oratory or pamphleteering) and they themselves wrote articles for which they could have been arrested. None of them saw Robespierre as any more of a political criminal than the English Prime Minister, William Pitt. Robespierre, said one of their circle, was 'a ministering angel, sent to slay thousands that he might save millions'.

When Coleridge lectured on politics in Bristol in 1795 he certainly had the reputation of a Jacobin – a revolutionary enthusiast – but his published lecture, 'Conciones ad Populum', is in fact a philosophical consideration of the violent excesses of revolution. Robespierre, he argues, meant well: 'I rather think, that the distant prospect, to which he was travelling, appeared to him grand and beautiful; but that he fixed his eye on it with such intense eagerness as to neglect the foulness of the road.' Unfortunately, such power as Robespierre possessed 'shapes and depraves the character of the possessor'. He concludes that there is an appalling connection between political **idealism** and political crime: 'If we clearly perceive any one thing to be of vast and infinite importance to ourselves and all mankind, our first feelings impel us to turn with angry contempt from those who doubt and oppose it. The ardour of undisciplined benevolence seduces us into malignity.' In his *Political Justice* (1793; see Historical Background) William Godwin had argued that mankind should cultivate universal benevolence rather than private attachments. Coleridge's lecture retorts that such attachments nurture philanthropy. 'The paternal and filial duties discipline the heart and prepare it for the love of all mankind. The intensity of private attachments encourages, not prevents, universal benevolence.' Out of this conviction grows the theme of friendship in the conversation poems. Coleridge's poetic disavowal of support for France, in 'France. An Ode', was written in February 1798, immediately following the first invasion of Switzerland. In April he wrote to his brother: 'I have snapped my squeaking baby trumpet of sedition ... I wish to be a good man and a Christian, but I am no Whig, no Reformist, no Republican.' He goes on: 'I have for some time past withdrawn myself totally from the consideration of immediate causes, which are infinitely complex and uncertain, to muse on fundamental and general causes.' Some have read *The Ancient Mariner* as a symbolic statement of this change of emphasis.

His poem 'Fears in Solitude', written in April 1798 when a French invasion was feared, is more patriotic than revolutionary, but Coleridge never became an unthinking patriot. His journalism in 1796–7 remained strongly anti-government. And in a letter of 23 March 1801 to Thomas Poole he was still contemplating emigration to America – not in search of Utopia, but out of disgust for 'the state of my poor oppressed country' where 'the laborious poor are dying with grass in their bellies'. He laments 'our pestilent commerce, our unnatural crowding together of men in cities, and our government by rich men'. And one of Coleridge's most powerful political statements was a lecture on the evils of the slave trade, and an appeal for a boycott on sugar, the major product of West Indies' plantations.

In later years Coleridge's was a conservative voice, but the poems treated in this Note mostly belong to Coleridge's radical years. And in these poems there are certain commitments – to the notion that God is found in Nature, that Nature is libertarian, that active benevolence is a major virtue, that human experience is social – which would have labelled him as a radical and a seditionist. The absence of obeisance to church and king, and the violence of his frequent outbursts against property, persecution, slavery and priesthood, make his a fiercely democratic poetry. 'Fire, Famine, and Slaughter', especially, with its savage **satire** on the war crimes of the Prime Minister, William Pitt, its thumping four-stress line, and the refrain screamed out by each spirit in turn – 'Létters fóur do fórm his náme' – has all the liveliness of the scurrilous, lampooning politics of the 1790s. Pitt, the poem says, is simply unspeakable.

THE INDIVIDUAL & THE POET

The purpose of life, says Coleridge, is to produce 'the highest and most comprehensive individuality' (*Theory of Life*), so 'every state of life which is not progressive is dead or retrograde' (*The Friend*). Most Romantic poets believed – at least in their youth – that the way to realise the best potential in human nature is not through repression of whatever is individual, eccentric and unconventional, but through liberation of human energies. One should follow one's impulses wherever they lead, for each individual is capable of creating new forms of order and beauty, new possibilities for humanity. The Romantic fascination with the spontaneity of the child is based on a widespread sense that each new human being is both uniquely gifted, and a new beginning for humanity: perhaps, Coleridge suggested, 'genius' is defined by the gift of preserving the fountain-like gifts of childhood into adult life. Whereas eighteenth-century culture emphasised tradition and socialisation, learning from the past, Romanticism emphasised experiment: the child may have new insights which adulthood should heed. Alexander Pope expressed the eighteenth-century ideal of a good poem as 'What oft was thought but ne'er so well expressed'; the Romantic poet seems to feel charged with expressing matters that were never thought or felt before, so as to enlarge the range of human experience. For that reason he is willing to listen to the promptings of the least conditioned, least habitual impulses of his being.

If Romantic poets share one ethical belief it is in the duty of self-development. As Thomas Carlyle (both a late Romantic and a Victorian prophet) put it: 'The meaning of life here on earth may be defined as consisting in this: to *unfold yourself*' and he cites Coleridge as an authority: 'Coleridge beautifully remarks that the infant learns to speak by this necessity it feels.' The characteristic Romantic poem, therefore, shows its hero, often the poet, in the process of discovering something about the world or himself, or in the process of becoming. Ideally, the poem will be both a growth experience for the poet, and a sort of vicarious growth experience for the reader.

We all sleep, dream and love; we experience anxiety, have moments of epiphany and moments of dread. We don't all have an acute fascination with how memory, and the unconscious, and perception, and impulse, and imagination function. The Romantic poem specialises in laying bare these moments in the experience of a unique human subject. As a poem by Robert Browning puts it, the function of the artist is not to reflect what we already think, but to *lend his mind out* so that we have the experience of seeing differently. He was, perhaps, enlarging on one of Coleridge's insights into the function of poetry. One function of the poetic imagination, says Coleridge, is 'so to represent familiar objects as to awaken the minds of others to a like freshness of sensation concerning them'. If that is the function of poetry, it may follow that the poet has a duty to communicate what emerges uniquely from his own fresh and individual experience of the world.

THEMES IN *THE RIME OF THE ANCIENT MARINER*

We can see how difficult it is to keep Coleridge's interests separate by looking at the way *The Ancient Mariner* has been interpreted. Robert

Penn Warren in his essay 'A Poem of Pure Imagination' (1945) commented very sensibly that Coleridge's description of this poem as a 'poem of pure imagination' does not mean it is meaningless. On the contrary it implies a poem which engaged the whole creative mind and soul of its creator, and which is likely to communicate a revelation of the meaning of life.

The themes of the poem, according to Warren, are: (a) the theme of sacramental vision, or the one life, and (b) the theme of understanding versus imagination. These themes are united in that the Mariner's daylight consciousness, associated with the burning sun, exhibits the 'world of death' which is all the understanding leads to, whereas his imagination, liberated under the moon, reveals the beauty of 'the one Life'. Many critics have wondered whether the poem is quite so consistent as that, but it has usually been interpreted along similar lines as a dream or nightmare version of the basic Christian drama of sin, repentance and salvation, adapted to the Romantic sense of the 'one Life' and the holiness of all that lives.

Other readers have found other themes, of course, especially ones which derive even more directly from Coleridge's personal life. In some ways his narrative poems are made of materials which are quite as personal to him as the immediately personal 'confessions' of the conversation poems. The central drama of transgression obviously relates closely to Coleridge's own fear of being damned for some involuntary sin – or simply because of original sin, which is perhaps the same thing. Coleridge believed firmly in original sin, and said that 'A Fall of some sort or other ... is the fundamental postulate of the moral life of man'. It is clear that the Albatross has Christian, or Christ-like, associations. Perhaps the Mariner demonstrates his share of 'original sin' in his self-destructive urge to kill what might save him, just as mankind crucified Christ, the Redeemer. But a specifically Christian reading raises all kinds of problems: the spirits at large in the world of the poem do not generally feature in the Christian world view, and the fate of sinners does not depend on a throw of dice aboard a phantom ship sailed by death and the nightmare death in life.

The dread of loneliness was also felt acutely by Coleridge. George Whalley's essay on the poem explores a number of its autobiographical aspects, and there is no doubt that the remarkable lines expressive of isolation are very personal: 'O Wedding-Guest! this soul hath been/ Alone on a wide wide sea: / So lonely 'twas, that God himself / Scarce seemed there to be' (lines 597–600). One can also take the poem as in some sense expressive of Coleridge's fears that he might slay in himself some quality which might be symbolised by the Albatross – whether that is the religious state of Grace, or the poetic gift of Imagination, which poets often symbolise in some majestic bird (Blake's Eagle, or Yeats's Swan). On that reading it is a sort of prophecy of 'Dejection: An Ode'.

Equally one can read the poem as a central Romantic myth, a treatment of the archetype of the Wanderer, or the Wandering Jew, Ahasuerus, who mocked Christ, and was condemned to wander the earth until the Day of Judgement. His story is reflected in Wagner's opera of *The Flying Dutchman*. The Mariner combines the motifs of these legends, 'passing like night from land to land', and doing eternal penance for some thoughtless crime against the principle of life itself. Yet Romantic art is ambivalent about acts of trespass, or 'fall', or defying the cosmic order. In some ways the Mariner is distinguished and elevated by his crime, which involves him in visionary experience beyond that which is available to the ordinary men who accompany him.

Here are seven ways in which various readers have seen the essential meaning of *The Ancient Mariner*. Your own interpretation may not be identical with any of these, or it may combine elements of them all. The poem has been seen as:

- an **allegory** of the fall, purgation and salvation, of the individual or of the race
- a myth expressing the Romantic belief in the 'the one Life'
- a symbolic expression of how **imagination** reveals spiritual realities which cannot be grasped by understanding alone
- a dramatisation of Coleridge's deep sense of sin, and the nightmare of being damned for some wholly involuntary action
- a nightmare voyage into the irrational, akin to a nightmare of inexplicable and inescapable guilt and suffering
- a parable, in which one man's exceptional crime and exceptional experience are rewarded by greater consciousness and vision into the meaning of existence
- a parable about the role of the poet and the human cost of being gifted with strange powers of speech

For many readers, the slaying of a sea-bird is simply not a sufficient crime in itself to justify the whole corrective supernatural apparatus that is brought to bear on the Mariner. The act must symbolise something else, perhaps the huge burden of historical guilts acquired by a nation which was engaged in such indefensible aggressive acts as the slave trade, imperialism and war. Perhaps, even, the imperial and loveless will of one man, a Robespierre or a Pitt, consigning his companions – even 'my brother's son' – to death.

GENIUS & JOY IN THE DEJECTION POEMS

A remark in Coleridge's *Philosophical Lectures* helps to explain why, in these poems, he associates poetic genius and joy. 'In joy individuality is lost and it therefore is liveliest in youth', before the hardships of life make men self-centred:

> To have a genius is to live in the universal, to know no self but that which is reflected not only from … our fellow creatures … but from the flowers, the beasts, yea from the very surface of the waters and the sands of the desert. A man of genius finds a reflex to himself, were it only in the mystery of being.

Genius and Joy are interdependent; both imply participation in the divine harmony of life. The doctrine of these poems is clarified by this comment. In the poetry there appears to be a contradiction between the thought that joy is given, and the thought that 'we receive but what we give, / And in our life alone does nature live' (lines 47–8 and lines 295–6). A reader could reasonably be expected to understand the latter to mean that the life of nature is a mere projection of the mind, and the beauty of nature is simply a reflection of the soul. The key, perhaps, is to see that what conditions the 'gift' of joy is a response to 'the mystery of being', a power of reciprocating: one cannot receive if one does not give, but that does not invalidate the 'gift'. Similarly, one could argue, nature does 'live', but is only felt to do so by those whose lives are responsive – who do not, whether in grief, dejection, or in the exercise of merely scientific understanding, cut themselves off from union.

In both poems there is of course the **paradox** that Coleridge is mourning the loss of his 'genial' spirits in a poem which demonstrates high powers of creativity. He also claims not to feel the beauty which he so beautifully evokes in the opening lines. Given his theme, he has a tactical problem: he must make us feel what he has lost, while suggesting his own detachment. How do the first fifty lines of the Letter (lines 1–46 of the Ode) do this?

The most imaginative observation in the opening passage is the one quoted from the ballad. Coleridge's own comments tend to be descriptive rather than **metaphorical**, and his mind seems to wander from the present scene, wishing indeed for a different scene. His preoccupation with his own problems is to some extent reflected in the rather detached air of his description: the observations are somewhat clinical, noting the sky's 'peculiar tint of yellow green' or the 'flakes and bars' of the clouds. If you compare the detail of these lines with the sense of involvement one finds in 'This Lime-Tree Bower' (lines 13–19 and lines 68–76), or the cluster of active images in 'Frost at Midnight' (lines 65–74), you will probably agree that, by comparison, 'that green light that lingers in the West' has a melancholy touch. The **ode's** first metaphor of unity is 'wedding-garment' in line 49, and that positive note is immediately cancelled by the following 'shroud'.

A similar sense of alienation comes out in the use made of the poem's main symbol, the lute. Whereas in 'The Eolian Harp' Coleridge seemed content to imagine himself as the harp, producing music as the breeze sweeps over him, here he rejects this view of the poet. The true poet is not like a harp, being played by the breeze; Coleridge could only be content with that **image** when he was a necessitarian, before he rejected Locke and Hartley. Now his image for the freedom of the true poet is the wind itself. So although in the seventh **strophe** of the ode there is a marked change – the long-awaited 'impulse' *has* arrived to change the mood – Coleridge still projects himself as excluded from the creative impulse: he is the listener, not the harpist.

FORMS & TECHNIQUES

THE CONVERSATION POEMS & ORGANIC FORM

'This Lime-Tree Bower My Prison', 'Frost at Midnight' and 'The Nightingale' are the finest examples of a form Coleridge invented: the conversation poem, or poem of friendship. 'The Eolian Harp' also belongs to this group, and 'Reflections on Having Left a Place of Retirement', 'To William Wordsworth', 'Fears in Solitude', and the verse 'Letter to — [Sara Hutchinson]' share some of the characteristics of the form. The critic G. M. Harper was the first to apply the term 'conversation poem', which Coleridge uses only in 'The Nightingale', in this wider sense. Other critics prefer to include these poems in a broader group which M. H. Abrams calls 'the greater Romantic lyric' (G. M. Harper's essay 'Coleridge's Conversation Poems' appears in *English Romantic Poets*, ed. M. H. Abrams). At first sight these poems may seem shapeless and even pointless: they don't rhyme, they don't have stanzas, they don't have a very obvious plot, and it almost seems that they could start and finish anywhere. But modern critics have seen them as exemplifying the Romantic principle of **organic form**

In his *Lectures on Shakespeare* Coleridge distinguished between 'form', which develops organically from the content of a poem, and which in some sense is implicit in the idea which gives rise to the poem, and mechanical 'shape' which is imposed on the content of a poem:

> The form is mechanic when on any given material we impress a predetermined form, not necessarily arising out of the properties of the material, as when to a mass of wet clay we give whatever shape we wish it to retain when hardened. The organic form, on the other hand, is innate; it shapes as it develops itself from within, and the fullness of its development is one and the same with the perfection of its outward form.

As Coleridge said in *Aids to Reflection*, poems like plants originate in seeds. A work of art grows, as a plant grows, from 'an antecedent Power or Principle in the Seed'. It chooses its own 'appropriate form'. **Organicism** was one of the key ideas of the Romantic age. Coleridge's view of literary organic form, itself taken from a German critic August Wilhelm Schlegel, is also comparable with a comment by Hegel who said that in 'a mature philosophy … just as in a living individual one life, one pulse beats through all its members'.

THE CONVERSATION POEMS AS GENRE

Albert Gerard, in a famous essay on 'The Systolic Rhythm: the structure of Coleridge's Conversation Poems' used an organic **metaphor** drawn from the human body to describe the way in which the consciousness in the poems expands and contracts. The poems display a rhythm, like the systole and diastole of the heart-beat, so that although each poem is rooted in the particularities of place, and Coleridge's physical being, it moves inwards to explore the inner mind of memory and imagination, and outwards to embrace the cosmos.

Apart from this organic rhythm, the conversation poems share a number of other characteristics:

They are written in the style of intimate talk to an understanding listener. For instance, 'This Lime-Tree Bower' opens with an exclamatory 'Well'; the repetitions and clumsy grammar in lines 4–10 suggest an unedited thought process, and the structure of the sentence in lines 10–16 is created by a natural series of recollections; he mutters an excited 'Yes' in line 26; he gestures towards objects, as in 'that walnut-tree' in line 51.

In most cases we know who the imagined addressee is. The poems are addressed to his wife (early in their marriage), to William and Dorothy Wordsworth, to Charles Lamb, to his son Hartley, and to Sara Hutchinson. This is far from being a formal gesture, like many dedications in poetry. Coleridge had a great gift for friendship, and a great need for it. He wrote in a letter: 'Man is truly altered by the coexistence of other men; his faculties cannot be developed in himself alone, and only by himself.'

In discussing **lyric** poetry we usually speak of a 'lyric persona': it is a safe rule not to assume that the speaker is the poet. In these poems, however, it is hard to avoid the impression that the speaker really is Coleridge himself (even if it is Coleridge playing a role): the consistent presence of his own many-sided identity is one of the distinguishing features of the conversation poems. Furthermore, we know the precise biographical context of the poems, sometimes because we are explicitly told what the context is, and sometimes because it is easily inferred.

Each poem gives a precise specification of space and time. Sometimes the place and date of composition are stated: this habit was shared by all the Romantic poets, as in Shelley's 'Stanzas written in Dejection near Naples', or Wordsworth's 'Lines written a few miles above Tintern Abbey on revisiting the banks of the Wye during a tour, July 13, 1798'. Coleridge specifies the time of day, the atmosphere, his exact surroundings, so that each poem has an easily visualised setting. It is not that he wants a picturesque frame for his meditation. Rather, the landscape, or fireside, or nocturnal sounds, or garden sights, stimulate the meditation that takes place and influence the direction his thoughts take. When a dramatic change occurs in the course of the poem it may be caused by some train of association in the poet's mind, or by a freak of memory, or by something outside him altogether: both inner and outer worlds are partners in the process. Coleridge thought of art as 'the reconciler of nature and man'. In these poems he reconciles 'what is nature with that which is exclusively human'.

This naturalness does not make the poems random or artless. Usually they have a satisfying shape – in the sense that the movement of thought circles or spirals around a given theme or image, while recording some kind of progress, either in insight or in the release of emotional pressure. Coleridge thought that 'the aim of narrative is to convert a series into a whole, and to make events which … move in a straight line, assume to our understanding a circular motion – the snake with its tail in its mouth' (Letter to Joseph Cottle, 7 March 1815). Usually the conversation poems come full circle at the end, recycling the opening imagery with added significance or subtle variation.

THE NARRATIVE POEMS

Coleridge recalls in (*Biographia Literaria*, Chapter 14, how the *Lyrical Ballads*' project was conceived by Wordsworth and himself. Wordsworth's poems were to be devoted to 'awakening the mind's attention from the lethargy of custom and directing it to the loveliness and the wonders of the world before us; an inexhaustible treasure, but for which, in consequence of the film of familiarity and selfish solicitude, we have eyes yet see not, ears that hear not, and hearts that neither feel nor understand'. His own endeavours, it was agreed 'should be directed to persons and characters supernatural, or at least romantic; yet so as to transfer from our inward nature a human interest and a semblance of truth sufficient to procure for these shadows of imagination that willing suspension of disbelief for the moment, which constitutes poetic faith'.

Of the five poems which Coleridge contributed to *Lyrical Ballads*, only *The Ancient Mariner* was a **ballad**, and it is really this poem which his words here describe. Coleridge wrote that had he finished *Christabel* he would have fulfilled his 'ideal' of a poem dealing with supernatural events far more successfully than in *The Ancient Mariner* (*ibid.*), though elsewhere he spoke of wishing to desynonymise the supernatural (that which is above nature) from the preternatural (that which is outside nature). In 1800, however, he agreed to exclude the two-part poem from *Lyrical Ballads* on the grounds that 'it was in direct opposition to the very purpose for which the *Lyrical Ballads* were published'. Part of that purpose, at least as Wordsworth conceived it in 1800, was to counteract the public thirst for outrageous and **Gothic** incident in poetry by demonstrating the deeper interest of the ordinary human passions.

NARRATIVE TECHNIQUE IN *THE ANCIENT MARINER* & *CHRISTABEL*
All three of Coleridge's 'visionary poems', 'Kubla Khan' (treated in Part Four), *The Ancient Mariner* and *Christabel*, are compound texts. 'Kubla Khan' is a bewildering combination of preface, vision and dream: its preface, last written, is the only key to the relation between the opium dream of Xanadu and the vision of the Abyssinian Maid. In *The Ancient Mariner* (1817 version) we have a fictional prose meditation which purports to be interpreting the poem itself. In *Christabel* readers have found a radical shift in narrative perspective between Parts 1 and 2, together with a real instability of genre throughout the poem, and the two 'Conclusions' are of course on entirely different planes. Each of these devices seems designed to complicate, or frustrate, the task of interpretation.

   The Ancient Mariner takes place on two thresholds. There is the literal threshold of a wedding feast (which follows a sacrament of marriage, which is itself a central Romantic **metaphor** of unity or oneness), and there is the implied threshold of consciousness: the Wedding-Guest is mesmerised by the Mariner, and 'cannot choose but hear' the message the Mariner brings him from another dimension. Furthermore, much of the Mariner's tale takes place in a state of trance, and in part concerns acts (one of trespass, and one of love or 'blessing') which arise without conscious deliberation on the part of the Mariner. That is, the subject of the poem is partly the unconscious, and the poem begins with a particularly dramatic form of a characteristic Romantic moment: a dream-like confrontation in which something nightmarish intrudes violently into social normality, arresting the Wedding-Guest.

It is only near the end of the poem that we are made aware that the selection of the Wedding-Guest was not accidental: 'That moment that his face I see, / I know the man that must hear me, / To him my tale I teach.' But what if anything does he learn? One effect of the Mariner's tale is to cause the Wedding-Guest, in one of Shelley's phrases about imagination, to '*imagine* that which we *know*'. That is, to come to an inward awareness of something which he already knows in theory: in this case, (as W.J. Bate suggests) that 'there really is a moral universe that cannot be violated with impunity'. We may all feel that to be so, but as Coleridge said, 'truths are too often considered as so true that they lose all the powers of truth, and lie bed-ridden in the dormitory of the soul' (*The Friend*). It is this truth, of course, that the Mariner himself must constantly relive, perhaps until the 'message' that he can extract from it corresponds in a more adequate manner to the power of the tale itself.

Also, of course, the Wedding-Guest is important in another way. As listener, he represents us. Like Walton in *Frankenstein* and Lockwood in *Wuthering Heights* and Ishmael in *Moby-Dick* (except that each of these is the frame narrator) it is through his eyes that we see the Mariner, not at a distance, but at arm's length; and his interjections dramatise the emotional response which we are likely to feel at various stages of the poem.

Coleridge also introduced, in a late revision, the device of marginal **glosses**, which contribute to the effect of the poem and help to emphasise that it belongs to an unusual dimension of experience – one that has to be interpreted to us. In a poem in which the metre tends to hurry us along, and the plot is eventful and gripping, the scenes exotic and compelling, we may tend to read it unreflectingly. The glosses call our attention to matters of particular significance. At the beginning they simply summarise events; only the last gloss in Part 1 expresses a judgement. Some of them seem entirely superfluous. Some help to clarify the text. Some interpret the narrative from a more theological point of view than that of the Mariner. For instance, the phrase 'a dear ransom' (line 160) adds an emotive gloss to the Mariner's matter-of-fact narration at this point. The longer gloss at lines 263–6 intensifies the Mariner's experience by importing what is probably Coleridge's own response (at the time the gloss was added) to the beauty of the night sky, and his own sense of being excluded from its joyful harmony.

At other times the glosses interpret the poem in a way that suggests a **Neoplatonic** editor trying to make moral sense of (or impose a moral sense on) a poem which has no consistent moral framework. The style of the gloss is clearly suggestive of another frame altogether: but its function may be to invite you to participate in the process of interpretation. Coleridge wanted his readers to think about what was happening, rather than just be carried along; but it does not follow that the 'right' interpretative framework is that of the 'editor'. You may find it impossible to accept a Christian reading of a poem in which justice is so arbitrary, either because the slaying of a seabird condemns one man to everlasting torment and 200 men to agonising death; or because the fates of the Mariner and his shipmates are settled by a game of dice. Might the poem be a symbolic critique of predestination?

In a way, the gloss plays a similar function to the frame narrative in numerous **Gothic** tales, but without the tedious business of an editorial voice claiming that what you are about to read is an ancient manuscript discovered under mysterious circumstances (the preface to 'Kubla' can be seen as another form of this).

Christabel has also been claimed to be a poetic response to numerous Gothic novels Coleridge had been reading, and reviewing, by such authors as Mrs Radcliffe and Matthew 'Monk' Lewis. Charles Tomlinson (whose essay appears in the Macmillan Casebook) examines the poem as a refined tale of terror, an exercise in poetic heightening of the Gothic, designed to explore the classic elements of the mysterious castle and the victimised and defenceless heroine, at a deeper and more psychological level than in the pulp fiction of the day.

But is Coleridge in fact attempting a Gothic poem? If it is an exercise in Gothic it is not at all surprising that it was excluded from the 1800 edition of *Lyrical Ballads*. But some have found its strange tone remarkably close to Wordsworth's counter-Gothic strategies in 'The Idiot Boy' and 'Simon Lee', poems which parody the Gothic and humanise it. The curious mannerisms and uncertainties and anxieties of the intrusive narrator, the comically 'toothless' mastiff bitch, the narrator's awe at such narrative clichés as the owls, Geraldine's inability to cross the threshold, the suddenly awakening fire, may well support

more interesting than typical gothic

such readings. More deeply, why does Coleridge deploy *apparently*
stereotypical figures, ultra-innocent and demoniacal, and then make it
increasingly hard for the reader to remain content with the narrator's
clear desire to interpret them in this way? *Christabel* plays strange games
with genre, and brings the reader face to face with his or her assumptions
and reading practices, long before its second conclusion turns into a
conversation poem, shatters the illusion, and bridges the gap between the
preternatural and the everyday.

other piece switcher

    Like 'Kubla Khan', also, *Christabel* may be designedly a 'fragment'.
Charles Lamb, always an insightful critic, declared that he had no desire
to see the poem finished, since any resolution of the plot would inevitably
destroy its mystery, yet other nineteenth-century readers debated a
variety of projected endings, all attributed to Coleridge, who usually
claimed that the poem was to have been in five cantos. Wordsworth
believed that Coleridge had no idea how he was going to finish the poem,
yet Coleridge circulated, via his son Derwent and his landlord Dr
Gillman, three versions of how it would have ended. One of these
variants (they are discussed by Humphrey House in an essay in the
Macmillan Casebook) suggests that we should not assume Geraldine to
be evil; rather she may be an agent of the spirit realm who has been
charged with a difficult task to perform. Two of the variants suggest that
Christabel has to suffer vicariously for the sins of her absent lover (her
name compounding Christ and Abel strongly suggests martyrdom). The
longest account suggests an action-packed development, with Geraldine
ceasing to impersonate the daughter of Lord Roland and assuming
instead the shape of Christabel's absent lover, before the said hero returns
and leads his betrothed to the altar. Such rumours play the same
destabilising role as the gloss in *The Ancient Mariner*. 'Kubla Khan' and
Christabel in their different ways challenge the reader to acts of **closure** as
well as interpretation.

3 alt endings.

THE DEJECTION POEMS

The completion of Christabel, and the composition of 'Dejection: An
Ode' and 'A Letter to — [Sara Hutchinson]' are almost the only
significant poetic products of Coleridge's move to the north of England.
Although a vigorous mountain walker he became increasingly sick from

rheumatic fevers, swollen leg joints, boils, nephritic pains, and a swollen testicle: his doctor treated him with leeches, poultices, ammoniac rubs, and – more pleasurably – Kendal Black Drop, a powerful form of opium. At the same time he subjected himself to a good deal of experimentation on sense perception, as an offshoot in his interest in preparing a refutation of the philosophical system of Locke, with the combined aid of Plato and Kant. In his own mythology of himself, these researches – combined with the virtual breakdown of his marriage – slew the poet in him. He was also by now in love with Sara Hutchinson. Feeling that both his creative life and his prospects of domestic happiness were over, he published his 'Dejection: An Ode' on the day of Wordsworth's wedding to Mary Hutchinson – an act which set the seal on his sense of exclusion.

Although these two poems are basically on the same subject, and one of them includes the other, there are distinct thematic differences. The usual view is that Coleridge first wrote the verse letter, and then edited from it the shorter **ode**, reducing 340 lines to 139, at a later date. The ode is seen as a censored version, more perfectly composed but less sincere. Whereas the published ode blames his failing creativity on 'abstruse research' and a declining capacity for joy, the longer poem appears to blame Sara Coleridge for driving him to that 'abstruse research', and associates his loss of joy with his hopeless love for Sara Hutchinson. This view has been challenged, however. George Dekker, in *Coleridge and the Literature of Sensibility* (1978), asks whether it is probable that so perfect an ode could be produced merely by cutting and rearranging a longer poem. He argues that long before 4 April 1802 Coleridge had been working on a version of the ode, and that both the letter and the ode are based on that earlier material. He also suggests that the ode is in some ways the more accurate poem, in that the letter, although more personal, is also more self-pitying. Coleridge wrote in his notebooks at the time he abandoned *Christabel* that 'Poetry is out of the question. The attempt would only hurry me into that sphere of acute feeling from which abstruse research, the mother of self-oblivion, presents an asylum.'

One reason for feeling that the ode may also be a more truthful poem than the more confessional one, is that Coleridge's real sense of guilt goes back to the time in 1799 when he stayed in Germany for three months after the death of his son Berkeley, doing his abstruse research and stealing from his own nature 'all the natural man'. Moreover, numerous letters, some of them long predating the breakdown of his marriage or his love for Sara Hutchinson, exhibit similar feelings of dejection. The probability is that to produce the apparently spontaneous 'Letter' Coleridge used some existing stanzas of poetry, interwoven with new passages (in verse of much rougher quality) to make a personal version for Sara Hutchinson and a few other friends.

Such information does not necessarily make one prefer one version to the other. Formally, the letter, with its extra lines, does not seem to have the unity or the dramatic power of the ode. For instance, its use of the 'wind-harp' image is less prominent, and the primary themes are slightly obscured by so much autobiographical musing. On the other hand, if a reader values poetry for its confessional quality, the letter is certainly richer, and it is valued more highly by many readers for that reason. As John Beer remarks, 'in order to hear the full throb of Coleridge's unhappiness the greater length of the earlier version is needed'. But is that what we go to poetry for? Coleridge the critic would have been appalled: yet his work did in a sense create the taste for Romantic self-exposure.

The Romantic assault on genre comes out very strongly in the strange relationship between 'Dejection: An Ode' and 'A Letter to — [Sara Hutchinson]'. Even though much of the ode is repeated word for word and line for line in 'A Letter', and one version of the letter has numbered **strophes**, nobody has ever called the letter an ode. One is a long confessional **lyric** poem; the other is one of the most perfect examples of a free form of Pindaric ode.

In 'Dejection: An Ode' Coleridge uses couplets and **quatrain** rhyme schemes, lines of varying length (from six to twelve syllables), **masculine and feminine rhymes**, and a variety of metres, to create a sense of the ebb and flow of feeling, or to mark 'transition in the nature of the imagery or passion' to use his own words. In reading it one must be ready to change pace and pitch at any moment. His handling of the shorter lines should be noticed especially: they are used either for effects of delicacy (''Tis of a little child / Upon a lonesome wild', lines 121–2) or to isolate a line of particular emotional force, for instance in referring to the moaning lute 'Which better far were mute' (line 8).

THE CONVERSATION POEMS

The conversation poem is a development of **lyric** poetry. The Romantic poets wrote innumerable formal lyric poems, but they favoured a hybrid form in which lyrical mood and subject are combined with **blank verse**, that is, lines of ten syllables each, in which the basic metre is **iambic** – alternating unstressed syllables with stressed:

To sít | be síde | our Cót, | our Cót | o'er grówn

Of course, no-one reads an iambic line as jerkily or as regularly as that, and it is unusual, especially in Romantic lyric poetry, to find many lines which are exactly iambic, even in theory. The first line of 'This Lime-Tree Bower' is not scanned as

Well théy | are góne | and hére | must Í | remáin

but (among several possibilities) as

Wéll,^ they are góne, ^and hére must I remáin.

Here the symbol ^ stands for a meaningful pause. In general you will find five stresses to an iambic line, but one or more of these may be silent, and may even occur between the lines. The only rule is: imagine yourself *saying* it to someone, rather than *reading* it to someone, and the lines will feel various yet balanced.

But the conversation poems are not always written in such relaxed cadence. In the early poems – 'The Eolian Harp', for instance – one sees interference from earlier verse styles. Lyrical blank verse is best when the units of sense do not coincide with the line endings; when, that is, the lines are 'run on', as they are in the first lines of 'Reflections' (line 7 is probably the only 'end-stopped' line in the first paragraph of that poem). In lines 26–33 of 'The Eolian Harp' – ironically, the lines added in 1817 – the verse (though fine and memorable) is formal in a rather eighteenth-century manner. The favourite verse for philosophical poetry in the eighteenth century was the rhymed **heroic couplet**, and when he added new lines to his poem Coleridge seems to revert to this older style. You will see that Coleridge has really written four unrhymed couplets (eight lines) in which the division of sense is made even more **rhetorical** by the use of elegant parallelism within and between the lines (this pattern is strongly felt in lines 34–43 and 54–7):

O the one life *within* us and *abroad* (antithesis)

Which *meets* all *motion* and *becomes* its *soul* (parallel nouns and verbs)

A *light* in *sound*, a *sound*-like power in *light* (chiasmus)

Rhythm in *all* thought and *joyance every where* (parallelism) (lines 26–9)

Lines 5 and 6 of the same poem illustrate similar elegance together with another legacy of earlier verse, the habit of using images as **emblems** of abstract qualities, here interpreted by Coleridge:

With white flowered Jasmin, and the broad-leaved Myrtle

(Meet emblems they of Innocence and Love!).

THE RIME OF THE ANCIENT MARINER

The verse form of *The Ancient Mariner* is a subtle modification of traditional **ballad metre** – a modification which Coleridge found in the ballad 'Sir Cauline' in Percy's *Reliques of Ancient English Poetry*. The norm is a four-line stanza, with alternating eight- and six-syllable iambic lines, rhyming on the second and fourth lines. But stanzas of five and six lines appear, and one stanza has nine lines. The five-line stanzas are made by inserting a couplet (rhyming lines 3 and 4), and many of the stanzas use strong **alliterations** and **assonances** or internal rhymes in the first and third lines: all three occur in line 75 'In mist or cloud, on mast or shroud'. Simple rhythmic repetitions can produce a stark sense of pain, as in

I closed my lids and kept them close,

And the balls like pulses beat

For the sky and the sea, and the sea and the sky

Lay like a load on my weary eye

And the dead were at my feet.

There are precisely two words of more than one syllable in this stanza, and they occur in the same position in lines 2 and 4 so that 'weary' echoes 'pulses', within a line already extending the mariner's torture (by the addition of those four extra 'beats' and the echoing of 'sky … sky' by 'Lay … eye'). Such variants appear at moments of particular tension, or when the pressure of the narrative delays the close of the stanza.

Nor is the number of syllables constant. Even the first stanza has irregularities in lines 2 and 3. But it is the accents or **stresses**, not the syllables, that count. To the eye, the third line of the poem has two extra syllables, but they do not upset the four-stress pattern of the line: we elide the shorter syllables into one: '(By thy) long grey beard and glitt(ering) eye.' Unlike the conversation poems, where it frequently seems right to replace expected stresses by a pause, the hypnotic quality of this metre is best realised by keeping to the regular alternation of three and four stresses to each line: 'Wáter, wáter, évery whére / Nor ány dróp to drínk.'

Part of the flavour of this ballad comes from Coleridge's use of occasional archaic terms, such as 'eftsoons', 'swound', 'weal', or outmoded pieties (outmoded in England anyway!) as in 'Heaven's Mother send us grace'. These add a sense of historical authenticity, although the language of the poem as a whole does not accurately reflect any actual period. Originally the poem was fuller of such archaisms to the point of quaintness. In revision, Coleridge kept just enough of them to differentiate his language from everyday usage, to create a sense of estrangement.

CHRISTABEL

Coleridge claimed in his preface to the poem that *Christabel* was based on 'a new principle, that of counting in each line the accents, not the syllables. Though the latter may vary from seven to twelve, yet in each line the accents will be found to be only four.' There are in fact a number of lines where there are only three, or even two (unless you are expected to say 'what | sees | she | there?'): but Coleridge expected his reader to realise that the poem contains half lines as well as full lines. In fact the principle was not 'new' but extremely old. He was really recovering, and turning to literary use, the accentual verse found in nursery rhymes (dúm, dúm, dúm de de dúm / the cát's run awáy with the púdding bag stríng) or the tendency of Anglo-Saxon verse to use two strong beats in each half line however many syllables there were. This requires one to pronounce words slightly against the grain of normal intonation. Just as in *The Ancient Mariner* ('Why lóokst thou só?' With mý cross-<u>bów</u>' / I shót the Álbatróss'), *Christabel* has lines which are heightened rather than casual: so that 'béautifúl excéedingly' really is a four-stress line. It is possible, by the way, that Coleridge's Devonshire ear naturally heard 'It ís an áncient máriné' as a four-stress line. He claimed that his own name was in triple metre (a very rare foot, an amphimacer) and should be pronounced Cóle-rídge). The same effect is heard in the chant-like balanced names of Le-o-line and Chris-ta-bel and Ge-ral-dine, which ensure that the lines end on a fourth stress.

SYMBOLISM

There is surprisingly little difference between the symbols used in Coleridge's most dramatic and his most intimate poems. One of his remarks about symbolism applies to all his poetry:

> In looking at objects of Nature while I am thinking, as at yonder moon dim-glimmering through the dewy window-pane, I seem rather to be seeking, as it were asking for, a symbolical language for something within me that already and for ever exists, than observing anything new. Even when that latter is the case, yet still I have always an obscure feeling as if that new phenomenon were the dim awakening of a forgotten or hidden truth of my inner nature. (*Anima Poetae*)

Nature, in Coleridge's poetry, can be minutely naturalistic, highly subjective, and yet plainly symbolic at the same time. That is, we see nature projected with sensuous clarity. We also see that the choice of objects, and the way they are used in Coleridge's meditation, makes them revelatory of his own states of feeling. And yet these same images, often moonlit or starlit, are of universal rather than private significance. For Coleridge the material world, however bright it may appear, is shadowy, in the philosophic sense that 'appearances' are the shadows, or reflections of 'ideas' projected on the flux of time. To use his own words, in the *Philosophical Lectures*: 'Plato ... conceived that the phenomenon [what is seen] ... is but a language by which the invisible ... communicates its existence to our finite beings'.

Coleridge habitually saw the world around him, especially the Lake District which he wrote about in vivid letters and notebook entries, in such terms. In a Letter of 1802, describing a waterfall near Keswick, he wrote:

> What a sight it is to look down on such a cataract! – the wheels that circumvolve in it – the leaping up and plunging forward of that infinity of Pearls and Glass Bulbs – the continual change of the Matter, the perpetual sameness of the Form – it is an awful image and Shadow of God & the World.

More formally, in *The Statesman's Manual*, Coleridge distinguished symbolism from **allegory**, in which meanings may be rather arbitrarily attached to images:

> a Symbol is characterised by a translucence of the Special in the Individual or of the General in the Especial or of the Universal in the General. Above all, by the translucence of the Eternal through and in the Temporal. It always partakes of the reality which it renders intelligible; and while it enunciates the whole, abides itself as a living part in that Unity of which it is the representative.

In this definition of symbolism (which has been vigorously challenged) is a clear illustration of Coleridge's belief that the visible world is symbolic of the invisible world, so that, as in 'Frost at Midnight', the objects we see are 'that eternal language, / Which thy God utters'. In Coleridge's view, poets do not symbolise their ideas; rather, the invisible world *symbolises itself* in the images we see.

PART FOUR

EXTENDED COMMENTARIES

TEXT **1** FRANCE. AN ODE

I

Ye Clouds! that far above me float and pause,
  Whose pathless march no mortal may control!
  Ye Ocean-Waves! that, wheresoe'er ye roll,
Yield homage only to eternal laws!
Ye Woods! that listen to the night-birds singing, 5
  Midway the smooth and perilous slope reclined,
Save when your own imperious branches swinging,
  Have made a solemn music of the wind!
Where, like a man beloved of God,
Through glooms, which never woodman trod, 10
    How oft, pursuing fancies holy,
My moonlight way o'er flowering weeds I wound,
    Inspired, beyond the guess of folly,
By each rude shape and wild unconquerable sound!
O ye loud Waves! and O ye Forests high! 15
  And O ye Clouds that far above me soared!
Thou rising Sun! thou blue rejoicing Sky!
  Yea, every thing that is and will be free!
Bear witness for me, wheresoe'er ye be,
  With what deep worship I have still adored 20
    The spirit of divinest Liberty.

II

When France in wrath her giant-limbs upreared,
  And with that oath, which smote air, earth and sea,
  Stamped her strong foot and said she would be free,
Bear witness for me, how I hoped and feared! 25
With what a joy my lofty gratulation
  Unawed I sang, amid a slavish band:
And when to whelm the disenchanted nation,

Like fiends embattled by a wizard's wand,
     The Monarchs marched in evil day,   30
     And Britain joined the dire array;
   Though dear her shores and circling ocean,
Though many friendships, many youthful loves
     Had swol'n the patriot emotion
And flung a magic light o'er all her hills and groves;   35
Yet still my voice, unaltered, sang defeat
     To all that braved the tyrant-quelling lance,
And shame too long delayed and vain retreat!
For ne'er, O Liberty! with partial aim
I dimmed thy light or damped thy holy flame;   40
     But blessed the paeans of delivered France,
And hung my head and wept at Britain's name.

III

'And what,' I said, 'though Blasphemy's loud scream
     With that sweet music of deliverance strove!
     Though all the fierce and drunken passions wove   45
A dance more wild than e'er was maniac's dream!
     Ye storms, that round the dawning east assembled,
The Sun was rising, though ye hid his light!'
     And when, to soothe my soul, that hoped and trembled,
The dissonance ceased, and all seemed calm and bright;   50
     When France her front deep-scarr'd and gory
     Concealed with clustering wreaths of glory;
       When, insupportably advancing,
     Her arm made mockery of the warrior's tramp;
       While timid looks of fury glancing,   55
     Domestic treason, crushed beneath her fatal stamp,
Writhed like a wounded dragon in his gore;
     Then I reproached my fears that would not flee;
'And soon,' I said, 'shall Wisdom teach her lore
In the low huts of them that toil and groan!   60
And, conquering by her happiness alone,
     Shall France compel the nations to be free,
Till Love and Joy look round, and call the Earth their own.'

IV

Forgive me, Freedom! O forgive those dreams!

  I hear thy voice, I hear thy loud lament,   65

  From bleak Helvetia's icy caverns sent –

I hear thy groans upon her blood-stained streams!

  Heroes, that for your peaceful country perished,

And ye that, fleeing, spot your mountain-snows

  With bleeding wounds; forgive me, that I cherished   70

One thought that ever blessed your cruel foes!

    To scatter rage, and traitorous guilt,

    Where Peace her jealous home had built;

      A patriot-race to disinherit

Of all that made their stormy wilds so dear;   75

      And with inexpiable spirit

To taint the bloodless freedom of the mountaineer –

O France, that mockest Heaven, adulterous, blind,

  And patriot only in pernicious toils,

Are these thy boasts, Champion of human kind?   80

    To mix with Kings in the low lust of sway,

Yell in the hunt, and share the murderous prey;

To insult the shrine of Liberty with spoils

  From freemen torn; to tempt and to betray?

V

    The Sensual and the Dark rebel in vain,   85

  Slaves by their own compulsion! In mad game

They burst their manacles and wear the name

    Of Freedom, graven on a heavier chain!

  O Liberty! with profitless endeavour

Have I pursued thee, many a weary hour;   90

  But thou nor swell'st the victor's strain, nor ever

Didst breathe thy soul in forms of human power.

    Alike from all, howe'er they praise thee,

    (Nor prayer, nor boastful name delays thee)

      Alike from Priestcraft's harpy minions,   95

  And factious Blasphemy's obscener slaves,

    Thou speedest on thy subtle pinions,

The guide of homeless winds, and playmate of the waves!
And there I felt thee! – on that sea-cliff's verge,
   Whose pines, scarce travelled by the breeze above,   100
Had made one murmur with the distant surge!
Yes, while I stood and gazed, my temples bare,
And shot my being through earth, sea and air,
   Possessing all things with intensest love,
   O Liberty! my spirit felt thee there.   105

Shelley thought this poem one of the finest of modern **odes**, although as a young idealist and enthusiast for revolution he lamented its repudiation of revolutionary politics, and along with 'Love' and *The Ancient Mariner* it was one of the most widely praised of Coleridge's productions. The very fact of calling a poem an ode (usually an elaborately wrought **lyric** poem of some length and in somewhat elevated language) announces the poet's intention of making a major 'statement', whether about the world or his art. Formally, this poem contrasts with the confessional 'Dejection: An Ode' (1802) which has a more musical structure made up of extremely varied line lengths and rhyme schemes to reflect its emotional instability. 'France. An Ode' has five stanzas of twenty-one lines in an exactly recurring rhyme scheme, which the indentations helpfully point out (*abba, cdcd, ee* followed by another **quatrain**, *fgfg*, and an intricate closing **septet** on three rhymes).

    The poem announces a major political shift by a writer who had been publicly identified for several years with pro-French politics. It also announces the Romantic theme of nature quite explicitly as an alternative to politics. If there is one single text which justifies the **New Historicist** enterprise (see Critical History) of refusing to take Romanticism at its own valuation as a literature committed to political liberty, it is this poem: here Coleridge openly redefines liberty as something which cannot be realised in political structures, but belongs to the individual – especially the Romantic poet? – in communion with clouds, waves and forests, 'inflamed with the love and adoration of God in Nature' (Coleridge, 'Argument', Oxford, p. 192).

    The poem is addressed at start and finish to 'Ye Clouds … Ye Ocean-Waves … Ye Woods'. The catalogue of **images** is conventional enough, and in general they behave conventionally enough – clouds float, birds sing, plants flower and the sun rises. The sky, however, 'rejoices' and Coleridge addresses all these natural forms collectively in line 18 as 'every thing that is and will be free'. He also calls on them as witnesses to his own worship of liberty. Liberty, by the way, is referred to as 'The spirit of divinest liberty' – a way of subtly acknowledging that the clouds, waves and trees are all responsive, as he will be at the end of the poem, to the wind as 'spiritus'. These natural forms 'Yield homage only to eternal laws' (line 4) which do not call upon them to behave unnaturally – unlike France's rulers.

What they are called to witness, as explained in the second stanza, is that at the start of the revolution he not only rejoiced, but was 'unawed' by the disapproval of the 'slavish band' of other Englishmen. When the monarchical powers of Europe, including Britain, tried to crush the revolution, even his patriotic feelings (lines 32–5) did not prevent him supporting the French: 'my voice, unaltered, sang defeat' to the enemies of France. Here Coleridge seems to be identifying himself with the brave and lonely Milton, who said in *Paradise Lost*, 'I sing ... unchanged' after the collapse of the English Revolution in 1660. Milton, who had been Cromwell's Foreign Secretary, and written a pamphlet justifying the execution of Charles I, was for Wordsworth, Coleridge and Shelley, the model of a politically engaged poet (and, of course the model of a poet who was also a legislator and the voice of his nation). Contrariwise, in one of his *Sonnets on Eminent Characters* Coleridge used the phrase 'with *altered* voice' (my italic) to express disapproval of Burke's critique of France. Is Coleridge half aware that he is now following in Burke's footsteps, rather than Milton's, and looking a little foolish?

The third stanza, or strophe, tries to lay the ghost of apostasy. Had he not been in the forefront of those who contested Burke's apostasy? To prove his loyalty to the cause of freedom he 'quotes' himself at the beginning and end of the third stanza making consistently staunch defences of France. First he claims that he initially looked on the blasphemies and other horrors of the Reign of Terror as a passing storm, behind which the Sun of Liberty was rising, using one of the commonest Romantic **metaphors** for the clouded revolutionary dawn. As Wordsworth, Southey and Thelwall had all done in 1794–96 (and Wordsworth would do again in *The Prelude*) he attributes France's warlike appearance (her 'front deep-scarr'd and gory' (line 51)) to outside interference and a legitimate need to crush 'domestic treason'. France has already been figured as a giant female (as in numerous **allegorical** paintings of Liberty in the Romantic era) stamping her foot and demanding freedom (lines 22–4): now she appears slaying the dragon of domestic treason. That this unfeminine role is forced upon her is implied by Coleridge's second 'speech' which looks forward to France comforting the poor, and exporting the revolution only by the example of her own domestic happiness.

The fourth stanza begins with a dramatic change: 'Forgive me, Freedom!'. Freedom is now identified with Switzerland, invaded and soon to be virtually annexed by imperial France. Why does Switzerland bring about such a revulsion of feeling? One reason is associated with the basic symbolism of the poem. Although Coleridge had not set foot in Switzerland, Wordsworth had, and he (as Shelley and Byron would do) shared the Romantic veneration of the Alps as the greatest and most sublime work of Nature and *therefore* the abode of freedom. Moreover, in the Romantic era the concept of 'national independence' and 'liberty' were virtually synonymous, many Romantic heroes and many Romantic literatures being associated with struggles against such continental empires as the Spanish, the Austro-Hungarian, the Turkish and the Russian. France, by invading the very home of peace, patriotism and liberty, and effectively annexing another nation, has become as bad as the worst of kings. There is a genuine ferocity in Coleridge's language in lines 80–84.

True liberty, the final stanza says, cannot be found in revolutions led by 'the Sensual and the Dark'. Liberty lives neither with the minions of Priestcraft nor with the slaves of Blasphemy. Coleridge, though still aligned with the religious 'left', as a Unitarian, now presents himself as occupying the middle ground, sharing the view of France as religiously benighted and lurching from one evil (Catholicism) to another, for which he uses .the rather vague term Blasphemy. The French revolutionary leaders were not, by and large, Atheists, but they were '**Deists**' who, Coleridge implies, had replaced the true God by a projection of human reason in such mock-religious events as Robespierre's Festival of the Supreme Being. The violence of Coleridge's feelings – and the gift for rhetoric he had displayed in his political lectures and journalism – comes out in his phrasing: 'factious Blasphemy's obscener slaves' (line 96). Up to this point the language of the poem has been elevated and impressive. The poem's guilt and anger blow themselves out in this storm of vituperation, and in the closing lines there is a sudden sense of release. The last septet is set off very clearly as announcing a new allegiance. There is a suggestion of the immediacy of the conversation poems as the section begins, 'And there I felt thee!' (line 99), sustained in the exclamatory 'Yes' (line 102) and the final line's 'O Liberty!' ('O Liberty' opens two lines in this final stanza: are they the same Liberty, or has she been reborn?) For the first time in the poem there is a sudden, and rather startling simplicity of language and freshness of imagery. The breeze, the pines, the distant surge of the sea, and 'earth, sea and air' are Liberty's real empire and Coleridge is her prophet. His human 'temples', perhaps, have replaced those of darkness and superstition and the false gods to whom so many have been sacrificed. It may be apostasy, but it is rather magnificent apostasy.

Yet this stanza announces what is, after all, a deeply despairing view of human liberty. As Coleridge's own summary explains, the ideal of Freedom, which 'the mind attains by its contemplation of its individual nature [the creative liberty of the mind] and of the sublime surrounding objects [the works of nature], does not belong to men, *as a society*'. Twenty-one years later, when Percy Bysshe Shelley rededicated poetry to the attainment of political liberty, he paid this poem the ultimate compliment. His 'Ode to the West Wind' similarly begins by addressing the 'unseen presence' of the wind, similarly describes the wind's power over the waves, the leaves and the clouds, but then takes a quite different tack: Shelley calls upon the wind to blow up the sparks of liberty and 'quicken a new birth' of revolutionary zeal.

TEXT 2   FROST AT MIDNIGHT

> The frost performs its secret ministry,
> Unhelped by any wind. The owlet's cry
> Came loud – and hark, again! loud as before.
> The inmates of my cottage, all at rest,
> Have left me to that solitude, which suits   5
> Abstruser musings: save that at my side

My cradled infant slumbers peacefully.
'Tis calm indeed! so calm, that it disturbs
And vexes meditation with its strange
And extreme silentness. Sea, hill, and wood,   10
This populous village! Sea, and hill, and wood,
With all the numberless goings on of life,
Inaudible as dreams! the thin blue flame
Lies on my low-burnt fire, and quivers not;
Only that film, which fluttered on the grate,   15
Still flutters there, the sole unquiet thing.
Methinks, its motion in this hush of nature
Gives it dim sympathies with me who live,
Making it a companionable form,
Whose puny flaps and freaks the idling Spirit   20
By its own moods interprets, every where
Echo or mirror seeking of itself,
And makes a toy of Thought.

                    But O! how oft,
How oft, at school, with most believing mind,
Presageful, have I gazed upon the bars,   25
To watch that fluttering stranger! and as oft
With unclosed lids, already had I dreamt
Of my sweet birth-place, and the old church-tower,
Whose bells, the poor man's only music, rang
From morn to evening, all the hot Fair-day,   30
So sweetly, that they stirred and haunted me
With a wild pleasure, falling on mine ear
Most like articulate sounds of things to come!
So gazed I, till the soothing things I dreamt,
Lulled me to sleep, and sleep prolonged my dreams!   35
And so I brooded all the following morn,
Awed by the stern preceptor's face, mine eye
Fixed with mock study on my swimming book:
Save if the door half opened, and I snatched
A hasty glance, and still my heart leaped up,   40
For still I hoped to see the stranger's face,

Townsman, or aunt, or sister more beloved,
My play-mate when we both were clothed alike!

   Dear Babe, that sleepest cradled by my side,
Whose gentle breathings, heard in this deep calm,   45
Fill up the interspersèd vacancies
And momentary pauses of the thought!
My babe so beautiful! it thrills my heart
With tender gladness, thus to look at thee,
And think that thou shalt learn far other lore,   50
And in far other scenes! For I was reared
In the great city, pent 'mid cloisters dim,
And saw nought lovely but the sky and stars.
But thou, my babe! shalt wander like a breeze
By lakes and sandy shores, beneath the crags   55
Of ancient mountain, and beneath the clouds,
Which image in their bulk both lakes and shores
And mountain crags: so shalt thou see and hear
The lovely shapes and sounds intelligible
Of that eternal language, which thy God   60
Utters, who from eternity doth teach
Himself in all, and all things in himself.
Great universal Teacher! he shall mould
Thy spirit, and by giving make it ask.

   Therefore all seasons shall be sweet to thee,   65
Whether the summer clothe the general earth
With greenness, or the redbreast sit and sing
Betwixt the tufts of snow on the bare branch
Of mossy apple-tree, while the nigh thatch
Smokes in the sun-thaw; whether the eave-drops fall   70
Heard only in the trances of the blast,
Or if the secret ministry of frost
Shall hang them up in silent icicles,
Quietly shining to the quiet Moon.

Most readers find this the most satisfying of Coleridge's 'conversation poems'. It illustrates perfectly what Albert Gerard meant by their 'systolic rhythm'. The meditation starts from a carefully created situation. From awareness of the night and the village setting – the speaker is almost alone but surrounded by family and community – we move into Coleridge's cottage, and a sense of his own restlessness, contrasted with the baby's quiet breathings. As he looks at the film on the grate he moves first into self-analysis, wondering why the film fascinates him – and, being Coleridge, he theorises this as a human need to find something companionable in one's surroundings. From introspection we pass to memory, as one 'film' dissolves into another, on the bars of the grate at school. Moving back, first to his schooldays in London, he remembers his homesickness. Moving further back into his childhood in Ottery, he encounters a memory of his baby sister, and this image allows a natural transition to the sleeping baby, Hartley, and his future. That future will be unlike his own past; it will have the Lake District, not London, as its environs, and so Hartley will be educated directly not by a stern preceptor but by 'that eternal language which thy God utters'. Having elaborated on this theme, he moves into the final paragraph or movement which first contemplates the seasons, and then homes in on the moment with which the poem opened, with the 'secret ministry of frost', now perceived as hanging up the water drops creating icicles which are 'Quietly shining to the quiet Moon'.

While this poetry us not so rhetorical as 'France. An Ode' nor as musical as 'Kubla Khan' it has its own artistry. In 'The **frost** performs its secre**t** minis**try**', like an artist deciding to paint a night picture using only blue and silver, Coleridge constructs a line in which all the important terms establish a particular set of sounds: sharp, **sibilant** and **fricative**. That miraculous first line creates a phonetic texture which is sustained all the way through the opening paragraph (and returns at the end). Underlying this, however, and less immediately noticeable perhaps, is another harmony: in 'per**form**s' and '**min**istry'. For whatever reason, it has been observed that meditative poetry often uses this sort of 'palette' when the theme of the poem is a fusion of inner and outer, material and spiritual. (In a famous line from Wordsworth's 'Tintern Abbey', his companion poem to 'Frost at Midnight', Wordsworth speaks of having felt 'a **sense sublime** / **Of something far more** deeply **interfused**').

In this case the sharp 's' and 'f' sounds and the soft 'm' and 'n' sounds unify not only the paragraph, but also the sharpness of the night and the quiet of meditation: phrases like 'abstruser musings', 'slumbers peacefully', 'vexes meditation', 'flaps and freaks', 'this hush of nature' and even barely noticed ones like 'have left me' or 'methinks, its', all carry this same texture. The silence is essential, and it is accentuated of course by the 'owlet's cry' so that the senses become stretched, almost enough to hear the inaudible, such as the 'silent ministry of frost', or the dreams of the nearby village, or the 'unquiet' film. Similar effects of language occur in the use or repetitions to evoke the yearning of memory, in 'how oft ... how oft ... as oft', or to enact the drowsiness of the day-dreaming schoolboy in 'dreamt ... sleep ... sleep ... dreams'. Greater energy comes from remembering the 'wild pleasure' of the bells of Ottery, described in a clause which runs for five whole lines without a pause.

Babyhood is the last image of the second movement, and this establishes the tenderness of the four lines evoking the 'conversation' that has been going on between the father's thought and the child's breathing (lines 44–7). The exclamatory 'My babe so beautiful!' introduces Coleridge's forward-looking and outward-moving thought, and there is a tumbling, excited quality to the imagined nature in which Hartley will grow up. He will have the freedom of the breeze (the image is quietly symbolic) and 'see and hear' the forms and sounds of the Lake District as 'that eternal language, which thy God / Utters'. 'Both lakes and shores / And mountain crags' and especially the clouds seem in this movement to be conscious of one another. The clouds seem to be exercising their own **primary imagination** as they 'image' the lakes and shores and mountains. This is emphatically a living and speaking universe, and nature has its own poetry.

Thus, Coleridge does need to overstate the final movement, in which he pulls off what may be the most brilliant and least showy symbol in all his poetry. Probably, when we read line 1 we did not ask what was signified by 'silent ministry', or even what the frost was doing. Now we see its work in the icicles, but we also know that icicles 'say' something. They are shining 'to' the moon as if speaking. What they shine with, of course, is moonlight, but this makes them equal with the moon itself, for it, too, reflects light from and to the sun. What we see in the icicle, at dead of night, is sunlight. One does not have to know that there are religions based on sun worship to feel that this symbol expresses perfectly the omnipresence of God: his light *and his heat* (Coleridge was enough of a scientist to know the immense difference between 32 degrees and absolute zero) present in an icicle at night.

But why 'quietly'? How else would they shine? Why, also, was the film of ash or soot the sole 'unquiet thing'? The film might have been agitated, as it is quite literally agitated by the draught of the chimney, but 'agitated' would have ruined the effect of that whole paragraph. In reading 'unquiet thing' we instantly dismiss the idea that 'unquiet' means noisy: rather it mirrors the poet's lack of quietude. The word is there perhaps, to hint at the absence of that quietude, preparing for its arrival at the close of the poem, when that other 'mirroring' takes place, which it will only do once the third movement has made clear, through another kind of mirroring, that we live in a symbolic universe.

France, of course, was not at all 'quiet' in 1798, nor Switzerland, nor was England, in the alarm of an invasion. Published with 'France. An Ode' and 'Fears in Solitude', 'Frost at Midnight' offers its quietude in a politicised context. After all, the poem itself reminds us that there are the poor to be thought of, in the Ottery bells which are 'the poor man's only music' and which fall on the ear like 'articulate sounds of things to come'. Might those things include justice? Is 'Frost at Midnight', perhaps, the final lines of 'France. An Ode' in a new key?

TEXT 3 KUBLA KHAN: OR, A VISION IN A DREAM A FRAGMENT

In Xanadu did Kubla Khan
A stately pleasure-dome decree:
Where Alph, the sacred river, ran
Through caverns measureless to man
   Down to a sunless sea.   5
So twice five miles of fertile ground
With walls and towers were girdled round:
And there were gardens bright with sinuous rills,
Where blossomed many an incense-bearing tree;
And here were forests ancient as the hills,   10
Enfolding sunny spots of greenery.

But oh! that deep romantic chasm which slanted
Down the green hill athwart a cedarn cover!
A savage place! as holy and enchanted
As e'er beneath a waning moon was haunted   15
By woman wailing for her demon-lover!
And from this chasm, with ceaseless turmoil seething,
As if this earth in fast thick pants were breathing,
A mighty fountain momently was forced:
Amid whose swift half-intermitted burst   20
Huge fragments vaulted like rebounding hail,
Or chaffy grain beneath the thresher's flail:
And mid these dancing rocks at once and ever
It flung up momently the sacred river.
Five miles meandering with a mazy motion   25
Through wood and dale the sacred river ran,
Then reached the caverns measureless to man,
And sank in tumult to a lifeless ocean:
And 'mid this tumult Kubla heard from far
Ancestral voices prophesying war!   30

    The shadow of the dome of pleasure
    Floated midway on the waves;
    Where was heard the mingled measure
    From the fountain and the caves.
It was a miracle of rare device,   35
A sunny pleasure-dome with caves of ice!

    A damsel with a dulcimer
    In a vision once I saw:
    It was an Abyssinian maid,
    And on her dulcimer she played,   40
    Singing of Mount Abora.
    Could I revive within me
    Her symphony and song,
    To such a deep delight 'twould win me,
That with music loud and long,   45
I would build that dome in air,

That sunny dome! those caves of ice!
And all who heard should see them there,
And all should cry, Beware! Beware!
His flashing eyes, his floating hair!   50
    Weave a circle round him thrice,
    And close your eyes with holy dread,
    For he on honey-dew hath fed,
    And drunk the milk of Paradise.

Despite Coleridge's elaborate introduction, few seriously believe that 'Kubla Khan' is unfinished. There is no difficulty in regarding the poem either as an entire text working with musical and symbolic logic, or as a wilful 'fragment', comparable to the kind of **Gothic** architectural folly popular in Coleridge's time, and all the more sublime because of its infinite suggestiveness. Most readers assume that Coleridge wanted readers to approach his text in a non-critical mood, or that he had some other ulterior motive for presenting it in this way. Some feel that the poem is so charged with eroticism (the woman wailing for her demon lover, the procreative chasm, the orgasmic fountain with its spermatic grains) that Coleridge felt he wanted to ascribe the composition to something beyond himself. Even the black 'damsel', whose arts are required to restore the poet's potency, fits into this scheme. Some think he wanted to excuse the poem's blasphemous potential (implied in the idea that the poet can lead us back to paradise, or build a dome which is not only superior to Kubla's but equal to God's holy city) so that the person on business from Porlock plays the same role as Sara in 'The Eolian Harp'. This fictitious person, therefore, adds to the poem's mystery as does the fact that Coleridge identifies the poem as belonging to not one but three Romantic genres: fragment, vision and dream. 'Dream' implies a creation of the unconscious (and the unconscious, Coleridge once said, 'is the genius in a man of genius'), and 'vision' implies a gift of God. Either way the poem is claiming to be the production of true genius unmarred by mere craft and the reflective understanding.

    Without the introduction, which alerts us to look for signs of an 'interruption', we would have little chance of detecting the poem's structure. It is made up of thirty lines of opium reverie, concerning Kubla

Khan's walled creation and the Romantic landscape which complements or threatens it, followed by six lines which seem to reflect on, or recollect, some scattered images from the vision and add the detail of the 'caves of ice', followed by a final movement in which Coleridge tries to persuade himself that if he could only remember an entirely different vision about a maid from another part of the planet he might be able to amaze the world by reconstructing Kubla's creation. (See David Perkins, 'The Imaginative vision of "Kubla Khan"', in J. Robert Barth & John L. Mahoney, eds., *Coleridge, Keats and the Imagination*, 1990, for an excellent discussion of these matters.)

Within this poetic structure we have two or three males from different dimensions of time and space (Kubla, the enchanted poet, and perhaps a demon lover), one or two females (the Abyssinian maid, who has nothing to do with Xanadu, and the 'woman wailing for her demon lover' who may only exist alongside the demon lover within a **simile** suggesting enchantment). We have a stately pleasure dome, and beautiful paradisal gardens 'here', and ancient forests, also 'here', and – within the walls or without them? – a deep romantic chasm, from which a sacred river bursts forth, only to disappear into a sunless sea. Is this savage chasm 'holy *and* enchanted' (my italic) because it is both at once or because it was *once* holy but is *now* enchanted, or might that depend on your religious point of view?

Despite the bewilderment created by these vertiginously 'there' and 'not there' images, there seems to be a musical progression. In the first movement, it has often been suggested, all is orderly and perhaps despotic – the verse is held together with insistent **alliterations** and **assonances**, **masculine rhymes** and powerful beats – and the dome is an attempt to defy time and destruction. In the second movement, all except the lines on the phallic fountain, and the final couplet returning to Kubla, have **feminine rhymes** and an extra syllable (the feminine 'chasm' disrupts the syllable count still more in two of them). Here nature is perceived as a perpetual cycle of creation and destruction, prone to orgasmic eruptions of the forbidden. In the third movement it may be implied by the now musing narrator that such domes are mere shadows cast on the flux of time. In the fourth the poet is inspired, or would be inspired (if only he could remember the tune), to build an Ideal dome, impermeable to decay, and harmonising the mingled measures of fountain and cave while reconciling sun and ice. To Coleridge, Imagination was capable of reconciling such polarities. Along with sun and ice other polarities include the river (of life?) meandering briefly between the fountains (of birth?) and the sunless sea (of death?), the wailing (dejected?) woman and the musical (joyful?) maiden, 'miracle' and 'device', and the dread aroused in the people by the ecstasy of the poet.

Would, could or should? All this is highly conditional. Could he revive the maiden's song, he would build a pleasure dome, which would be the same ('that dome'), yet not the same, for he would build it 'in air' and 'with music'. And could he do all this, with his 'flashing eyes, his floating hair' he should be revered or feared as a true prophet, unlike Kubla, perhaps, whose vision leads only to prophecies of ruin (as his fleet was wrecked on the shores of Japan). Moreover, the poet's music would enable all who heard to see what he imagines. Music is the purest vehicle of imagination, and imagination – in one of Coleridge's definitions – allows us to perceive the real behind this world of shadows.

Most nineteenth-century critics were content to read this poem as a piece of musical nonsense, enjoyable for its strange and sensuous imagery, and its fashionable orientalism, and its impressive and varied cadences (notice its mingling of iambic **pentameters**, iambic and trochaic **tetrameters**, and a solitary **trimeter** threatening us with the 'sunless sea'). It should certainly be enjoyed partly as verbal music, but does the intricate tapestry of sound make Coleridge's claims for the poem's unconscious composition more credible or less so? Along with the symmetry of 'i-a-a-u' and 'i-u-a-a' in the first line, the alliterations ending each of lines 1–5, and such echoes as 'pleasure' and 'measure', how many other assonances and internal rhymes are worked into the opening paragraph? You may feel that all this suggests careful art, not unconscious activity: yet babies alliterate before they can do anything else. The opening assonances chime with an infant's urgent 'mamma', and the first 'pleasure dome' is the breast: Kubla's erotic retreat was in several ways regressive.

Modern critics have tried to make sense of this poem in a multiplicity of ways, mostly making use of the research done by such scholars as J. Livingston Lowes, and John Beer and H.W. Piper as to the content of Coleridge's mind. This included Purchas's *Pilgrimage*, Bruce's *Travels to Discover the Source of the Nile*, Maurice's *History of Hindostan*, Bartram's *Travels through North and South Carolina*, numerous classical histories, Burnet's *Sacred Theory of the Earth,* which accounted for the appearance of mountains and caverns after the Fall, and Milton's *Paradise Lost*, with its conjecture that paradise was in Assyria on Mount Mazius, the source of the four rivers of Eden, including the (Ch)abora. He also knew:

- Ezekiel's prophecy of the rebuilding of Jerusalem, and his account of women wailing for the demon Tammuz in the valley of Lamentations
- St John's visions– in *Revelation* – of 'the river of water of life', flowing from the throne of God, and of a new Jerusalem suspended in heaven
- the myth of Isis searching to reassemble the dismembered Osiris, on the banks of the Nile, whose sources include the Abora
- the myth of Cybele, an earth goddess associated with both fertility and destruction
- the myth of Bacchus, the god of intoxication, who was nurtured on milk and honey.

Perhaps the poem is a kind of imploded epic, a poetic black hole of prophecies, myths and sacred texts forced into a startling unity. But does knowing what Coleridge read – even if one *could* know all that he read –lead to an interpretation? Coleridge's reading littered his mind with imagery, but how is it working?

Both Bruce's and Bartram's *Travels* described rivers originating in fountains, and in Bartram's case, returning underground. Both writers associate the explosive force of these fountains and their deluges with fragments of rock and trees. In Coleridge's time, fragments and torrents suggested apocalyptic furies. Might the war prophesied to Kubla have been the apocalyptic war then (1798) raging in Europe? Did Coleridge remember that Kubla was credited historically not only with warlike feats (like his grandfather Ghengis Khan) but with introducing Buddhism to his realm, as the result of a vision? Is there some connection with Coleridge's own shift from expecting the **Millennium** in 'Religious Musings' to recognising in 'France. An Ode' that only Milton's 'paradise within thee' is allowed to humankind? Is that why his dome is aerial rather than material? His vision does not, after all, include a restoration of Kubla's paradisal garden, with its echoes of Milton's (also walled) Eden. One possibility, then, is that this is, however obliquely, a political poem, a symbolic expression of political disenchantment and defeat.

Prolonged meditation over several hours may lead you to conclude that the poem contains within itself everything needed for an entirely satisfactory interpretation, whether you prefer to see the poem in psychological or political or mythological terms, or indeed as a statement about poetic imagination and the inevitable difference between aspiration (or inspiration) and achievement. Yet the next time you pick it up you may have to start again at the same point of bafflement. Like *Christabel*, this poem has successfully defied any critical consensus as to its meaning. In other words, whether Coleridge set out to do this or not, the poem offers the reader the experience it describes: that of not quite being able to hold on to what one thinks one sees. It is in the highest degree a *scriptible* or 'writerly' text, one written by the reader in the act of reading, and capable of suggesting quite different meanings each time one reads it.

PART FIVE

Background

Coleridge's life and work

Coleridge was born in Ottery St Mary, Devon, on 21 October 1772, the youngest of ten children in the family of John Coleridge, vicar and schoolmaster. After his father died when Coleridge was only nine, he was sent to Christ's Hospital, a famous charity school in London. His lifelong friend, the essayist Charles Lamb (1775–1834), was a fellow pupil, and later described him as 'the inspired charity boy' confounding his elders with his range of learning.

At nineteen, in October 1791, Coleridge entered Cambridge University, and began an erratic career, which included an episode in which he ran away and enlisted in the 15th Regiment of Light Dragoons, under the pseudonym of Silas Tomkyn Comberbach, and ended in December 1794, without taking a degree. In June of that year Coleridge walked to Oxford, where he met the poet Robert Southey (1774–1843). Together they conceived an idealistic project for emigration to America, to found a commune as an experiment in 'human perfectibility'. Coleridge called the scheme Pantisocracy. Property would be communal, and leisure time would be devoted to reading and philosophical discussion. In the summer of 1795 this plan collapsed, but it had one permanent effect. Robert Southey was engaged to Edith Fricker. In the interests of the Pantisocracy experiment, Coleridge became engaged to Edith's sister, Sara, whom he married in October 1795.

Coleridge soon moved to Bristol, writing and editing a political journal, *The Watchman*. When this failed, the Coleridges were helped by Thomas Poole, a prosperous businessman of liberal views, who raised funds to support Coleridge and his family (their first son, David Hartley Coleridge, was born in September 1796), and found them a cottage at Nether Stowey in the Quantock hills – still known as Coleridge's cottage. Here, in the spring of 1797, Coleridge began his friendship with William Wordsworth (1770–1850) and his sister, Dorothy; Wordsworth moved from Dorset to be near Coleridge. This was one of the most productive friendships in literary history. For many years, each gave the other the kind of support they needed. Coleridge had the finest audience a young philosopher could have – doggedly sceptical and hard to convince, but willing to let his brilliant friend talk away. Wordsworth had an admirer who not only saw him as a great poet but who could produce critical theories to prove it! In the presence of the Wordsworth household Coleridge produced most of his finest poetry, and much of his early philosophical writing. Late in the summer of 1798 appeared one of the most famous of literary collaborations, the *Lyrical Ballads*, generally regarded as the text which inaugurated English Romanticism.

Throughout 1797 Coleridge had been considering his career. In January 1798 he was preparing to become a minister of the Unitarian Church, and he preached a trial sermon in Shrewsbury, to a congregation which included the essayist and critic William Hazlitt (1778–1830). But at this critical point Tom and Josiah Wedgwood, the philanthropic sons of the founder of the famous pottery firm, offered Coleridge an annuity of £150 for life (an extraordinary sum in 1798 when Coleridge claimed his living expenses were about £90 a year) which enabled him to focus on writing. In May 1798 a second son, Berkeley, was born, and named, as was Hartley, after the philosopher Coleridge most admired at the time.

In September 1798 Coleridge and the Wordsworths left for Germany, where Coleridge studied philosophy and science at the University of Göttingen. Berkeley was taken ill in October and died in February after a long and painful experience of smallpox, which had infected Sara and Hartley too. News of this death and its effect on Sara reached Coleridge in March. He went on a walking tour of the Harz mountains, lingered a while longer in Göttingen, and finally returned home in July, to an irreparably damaged marriage and a mountain of guilt.

The Wordsworths, on their return to England, stayed for a while with the Hutchinson family near Durham in the North of England. Coleridge visited them there, and fell in love with Sara Hutchinson, beginning a long relationship which was both sad and inspirational: he wrote numerous love poems to the new Sara, known as the 'Asra' poems. William and Dorothy settled in Grasmere, in the Lake District, in 1800. Although increasingly estranged from his wife, Coleridge brought his family north to live in Greta Hall, in Keswick, some fourteen miles from the Wordsworths at Dove Cottage.

At first, Coleridge was happy in the new setting, and vigorous enough to become a serious fell-walker. Visits between the Coleridge and Wordsworth households were frequent: from Keswick to Grasmere is a thirteen-mile walk by the direct route, but Coleridge went via Helvellyn (3118 feet) on several occasions, as he did when he read them the second part of *Christabel*. But frequent illnesses made him more and more dependent on laudanum (liquid opium). He was also extending his philosophical and scientific studies in an experimental manner, subjecting himself to 'a multitude of little experiments on my own sensations and on my senses, and some of these (too often repeated) I have reason to believe did injury to my nervous system'. This injurious 'abstruse research' is referred to in 'Dejection: An Ode'.

He went to Malta for two years, as Public Secretary to the Governor, Sir Alexander Ball. But his health was no better, and his spirits were worse, when he returned to London in 1806. After eighteen nomadic months, partly in London (where he gave a course of philosophical lectures in January 1808), he returned to the Lake District. From August 1808 to May 1810 he shared the Wordsworths' new home at Allen Bank in Grasmere, and with Sara Hutchinson's help produced twenty-seven numbers of his periodical *The Friend*.

From 1810 to 1816, back in London, Coleridge's life was personally ruinous, yet remarkably productive. He gave several courses of lectures, wrote for newspapers, and saw his tragedy performed. He prepared an edition of his poems, *Sibylline Leaves* (1817) and began the composition of his literary autobiography, *Biographia Literaria* (also 1817), a milestone in literary criticism. In April 1816 a medical friend, Dr James Gillman, took charge of Coleridge and brought both his illness and his addiction under control. For the remainder of his life Coleridge was Gillman's house-patient. In 1824 Coleridge was made an associate of the newly established Royal Society of Literature, with a pension of £100 a year.

The greater part of Coleridge's philosophical and critical writing belongs to the Highgate period, including *The Statesman's Manual* (1817), *On Method* (1818), *Aids to Reflection* (1825), and *On the Constitution of Church and State* (1828). These late works, especially *Aids to Reflection* and *Church and State*, greatly influenced the rising generation of Victorians. He had a circle of disciples who came repeatedly to listen

to 'the sage of Highgate'. He died on 25 July 1834, in Highgate, where
he is buried.

HIS OTHER WORK

Even the work completed and published in his lifetime was impressive in
its scope, yet he was also celebrated as a journalist, as a lecturer, and for
his conversation. From these sources several generations of scholars have
edited the following posthumous works: *The Collected Letters*, edited by
E.L. Griggs, in six volumes; and five double volumes of the *Notebooks*,
and several volumes of commentaries on his reading, the *Marginalia*.
Other titles in the *Collected Works* (in addition to all the titles mentioned
above) include three volumes of *Essays on his Times*, his *Lay Sermons*, his
Table Talk, the *Logic*, and three sets of lectures, *Lectures 1795: On Politics
and Religion*, *Lectures 1808–19: on Literature*, and *Lectures 1818–19: On
the History of Philosophy*. Useful and more widely available compilations
from these works are *Confessions of an Inquiring Spirit* and *Anima Poetae*
(selections from his notebooks). A reconstruction of his legendary *Opus
Maximum*, from which all his other activities were lifelong distractions,
will soon appear – a work in which Coleridge desired to demonstrate the
necessary logical connections of the Christian religion and the entire
tradition of Idealist philosophy from Plato to Immanuel Kant.

HISTORICAL BACKGROUND

Coleridge's adult life spans the period from the French Revolution of
1789 to the First Reform Bill of 1832. When Coleridge was seventeen,
the Bastille prison was stormed by crowds in Paris; when he was twenty-
one King Louis XVI was executed, as was the revolutionary leader,
Robespierre, a year later. He was thirty-two when Napoleon became
Emperor, and forty-three when the Duke of Wellington and Marshal
Blücher defeated Napoleon at the Battle of Waterloo. He was forty-seven
when in 1819 an English crowd demanding the reform of Parliament was
fired upon by mounted soldiers: this incident, 'the Peterloo Massacre',
was a formative event in the lives of the next generation of Romantic
poets, Lord Byron (1788–1824) then thirty-one years old, Percy Bysshe

Shelley (1792–1822) and John Keats (1795–1821). The partial reformation of parliamentary franchise in England (the reform of constituencies and extension of the vote) was enacted when Coleridge was sixty. In the last year of his life, 1833–4, Parliament passed an Act preventing the employment of children under the age of nine, and another establishing the hated system of 'workhouses' for the poor; slavery was abolished in the British Empire, and a group of Dorsetshire labourers, the Tolpuddle Martyrs, were transported to Australia for illegally joining a trade union. The age began with clear-cut revolutionary issues and ended in a muddle of contradictory legislation.

The dominant fact of the early 1790s was, as Wordsworth expressed it in *The Prelude*: 'France standing on the top of golden hours / And human nature seeming born again'. If there were any young writers who did not share that enthusiasm, apart from Jane Austen, they have been forgotten. Edmund Burke, representing a conservative constitutional position, published his *Reflections on the Revolution in France* in 1790, but his eloquence had no effect, at the time, on Coleridge's generation: except astonishment that one of the great supporters of the American revolution should so bitterly oppose the French. In 1791, the year Coleridge entered Cambridge, Thomas Paine's *The Rights of Man* was published, to answer Burke's criticisms and, in effect, to argue for the establishment of a republic in England by revolutionary means if necessary. This work, which sold 1.5 million copies, helped to create a political opposition so fervent and articulate that the government of the day resorted to savage measures of repression. In 1792 Mary Wollstonecraft published her celebrated *A Vindication of the Rights of Woman* which, some argue, had an equally strong influence on Wordsworth and Coleridge. In 1793 William Godwin published his *Inquiry, Concerning Political Justice*. Godwin took a more philosophical approach than Paine, but his work is equally radical in its vision of the just society which it prophesied as the inevitable result of the evolution of man's reason.

The French Revolution led to very different consequences in reality. For the first three decades of the nineteenth century England suffered the consequences of the Napoleonic Wars. Democratic institutions had been undermined by the Government's war dictatorship. The growing cities of the Industrial Revolution were overcrowded with working families whose livelihood was threatened by mechanisation. The issue which dominated the 1820s and 1830s was parliamentary reform, and on that issue Coleridge played a more conservative role. What he wanted was not a parliament representative of the clamorous new industrial areas, carrying out 'the will of the people', but one which would balance what he now saw as three essential interests: 'permanence', or the survival of the aristocracy and gentry, 'progression', or commerce and the professions, and 'cultivation'. This last component Coleridge calls a 'National Church' or 'Clerisy' – by which he means those whose functions are spiritual and educational, and whose contribution is the pursuit of civilisation in its broadest sense.

LITERARY BACKGROUND

EIGHTEENTH-CENTURY POETRY

Romanticism reacted against the prevailing philosophy and sensibility of the eighteenth century, in which wit, reason, order and restraint prevailed. Eighteenth-century literature tends to be polished, commonsensical, socially assured and refined in tone and style. If the key term in the Romantic era was 'Imagination', that of the preceding age was 'Taste'. Yet Coleridge and his contemporaries were strongly influenced by some eighteenth-century ideas and literary models.

Wild, 'Romantic' landscapes had begun to appear in eighteenth-century verse. In 1757 Edmund Burke published his *Enquiry into the Origin of our Ideas of the Sublime and the Beautiful*. The Romantic poets would refine his psychology, but he too felt the power of vast or terrifying natural scenes to produce 'the strongest emotions which the mind is capable of feeling'. In poetry and the visual arts, sublime scenery was fashionable in the late eighteenth century.

Some poets of that period had also begun to enquire into man's relationship to nature in something of a Romantic spirit. For instance, the Reverend William Lisle Bowles (1762–1850) published a book of *Fourteen Sonnets* in 1789 which inspired Coleridge to write a **sonnet** in praise of him. What Coleridge admired in such poems as 'The River Itchin' (which he imitated in 'The River Otter') was Bowles's use of convincing natural **imagery**, his tenderness and his occasional **sublimity**. But he criticised Bowles's 'moralising' and his 'loose mixture' of natural images and moral analogies. Rather, he says, 'a poet's heart and intellect should be combined, intimately combined and unified with the great appearances of nature'. Similarly, Coleridge imitates and extends the work of William Cowper (1731–1800). Coleridge's 'Frost at Midnight' borrows a good deal of imagery and observation from a fireside scene in Cowper's long poem *The Task* (1784).

ROMANTICISM

Literary history classifies Coleridge as one of the great English Romantic poets, the others being Blake, Wordsworth, Byron, Shelley and Keats. The lifetimes of the major Romantic poets span the period between 1757, when Blake was born, and 1850, when Wordsworth died. Their most productive period runs from 1789, when Blake printed his *Songs of Innocence*, to 1824, the year of Byron's death and of the last cantos of his *Don Juan*. Modern anthologies tend increasingly to represent also the voices of such 'minor' poets (bestsellers in their time) as Charlotte Smith, Felicia Hemans, Helen Maria Williams, all of whom were admired by Wordsworth and Coleridge and forgotten by later anthologists. The change in emphasis from anthologies of Romantic poetry to Romantic period poetry is a necessary part of feminist reconfigurations of literary history in this period.

Numerous definitions of Romanticism have been offered. Common strands in such definitions include:

- A preference for imagination, myth and symbol
- A desire to overcome the division between man and organic nature
- An emphasis on the individual and the duty of unfolding the self
- A desire to overthrow all structures of oppression and division – of gender, race or class
- The discovery of the unconscious and the importance of dreams
- The creation of poetic forms which activate the imagination of the reader

Since Coleridge's poetry is always philosophical – 'no man was ever yet a great poet without being at the same time a profound philosopher' he once wrote – it is helpful to have at least a rudimentary map of his philosophical bearings.

Foremost of the philosophers who influenced Coleridge was Plato, the Greek philosopher (born 428BC). The founder of philosophical idealism, Plato also profoundly influenced Christian thought. His philosophy is a blend of reason and mysticism. He believed that nothing in the material world is permanent, or 'real'. Knowledge, therefore, is derived not from the senses but from reason. At the centre of Plato's thought is the concept of Ideas, or Forms. Behind each kind of 'appearance' in the world – a cat, a chair, a mountain – there is an Idea, eternally existent, and never wholly identical with any actually existing sample of these things. Without such an Idea, of course, conversation between human beings would be impossible – for every existing chair there would have to be a different term.

Like many other thinkers, Coleridge approached Plato through the Roman philosopher Plotinus (AD204–70). From St Augustine (345–430) onwards, Christian thought was largely built on Plotinus's representation of Plato's ideas – or **Neoplatonism**. Plotinus, like Plato, turned away, from the shadows of our world to contemplate a world of eternal goodness and beauty. Central to his world picture was the idea of 'God' as a spiritual triad made of 'the One, Spirit, and Soul. In this trinity, 'Soul' does not mean man's soul, but the creator of the visible world, a world which was, to Plotinus, beautiful and (as in *The Ancient Mariner*) inhabited by spirits. In England in the seventeenth and eighteenth centuries there was a native tradition of Neoplatonism, represented by such men as John Smith (1618–52) and Benjamin Whichcote (1609–88), the 'Cambridge Platonists'.

The dominant names in British philosophy are those of John Locke (1632–1704), George Berkeley (1685–1753), David Hartley (1705–57) and David Hume (1711–76), in whose tradition, says Coleridge, he could not find 'an abiding place for my reason' (*Biographia Literaria*, Chapter 9). Locke's *Essay, Concerning Human Understanding* (1690) argues that all knowledge is derived from sense perceptions – an idea to which Coleridge became wholly opposed as it denied intuition and imagination (or **Reason** as Coleridge uses the word). Along with

Locke's 'sandy sophisms' Coleridge came to dismiss the work of David Hartley. Hartley's *Observations on Man* (1744) is a mechanical description of the nervous system. When we perceive something, the nervous system 'vibrates': each vibration leaves a trace, a 'vibratiuncle', and the memory depends on these traces which, when reactivated, tend to reactivate each other. From associations of such sensory traces all our reasoning results. Hartley's world of vibrations and associations is given poetic expression in 'The Eolian Harp', and even in 'Frost at Midnight'. But in March 1801 Coleridge wrote 'I have overthrown the doctrine of association as taught by Hartley, and with it all the irreligious metaphysics of modern infidels – especially the doctrine of necessity'.

Instead, Coleridge turned to Germany to find philosophers who spoke his language. Baruch Spinoza (1632–77) was Coleridge's greatest temptation. To Spinoza there is only one substance, 'God' or 'Nature'. God is infinite and includes the attributes of thought and of extension. Everything that exists is an aspect of the divine. The aim of life is an increase in consciousness of oneness with 'God': one must free oneself from intellectual error and selfish passions in order to obtain both wisdom and happiness by seeing one's own life as simply part of the universal harmony. Coleridge soon diagnosed Spinozism as **Pantheism**, and rejected it as incompatible with Christian belief or with human freedom.

Immanuel Kant (1724–1804) was the greatest contemporary influence on Coleridge: his works, such as the *Critique of Pure Reason* (1781), 'took possession of me as with a giant's hand'. Kant's new Idealism was not identical to Coleridge's later views, but refuted successfully the ideas of Locke. Recognising the inadequacy of empiricism, Kant claims that the mind's knowledge of the world does not depend upon its being shaped by outer objects, but vice versa: objects conform to the structures of the mind. He asserts too (following Plato) that there are two kinds of knowledge: the partial knowledge we acquire through our experience of sense perception (Understanding); and the real knowledge of the intellect (Reason). Kant held that empirical reasoning does not supply moral values. The Understanding is competent to deal only with the material. In Kant, Coleridge found support for his view that if the wrong kind of thought is applied to morals 'the more strictly logical the reasoning is ... the more irrational it is'. We are assured by the very structure of the mind and the conscience (not by observable phenomena) that God, free will, intuition, the conviction of immortality, are essential postulates of the moral life.

PART SIX

CRITICAL HISTORY & FURTHER READING

NINETEENTH-CENTURY APPRAISALS

Nineteenth-century critics were agreed: the important Coleridge poems were *The Ancient Mariner*, 'Kubla Khan', and *Christabel*. Lamb found himself affected by *The Ancient Mariner* as by no other tale: 'After first reading it I was totally possessed with it for many days – I dislike all the miraculous part of it, but the feelings of the man under the operations of such scenery dragged me along like Tom Piper's magic whistle.' John Gibson Lockhart wrote of it in 1819 that 'above all the poems with which we are acquainted in any language – it is a poem to be felt – cherished – mused upon – not to be talked about – not capable of being described – analysed – or criticised. It is the wildest of all the creations of genius ... The loveliness and terror glide before us in turns – with, at one moment, the awful shadowy dimness – at another, the yet more awful distinctness of a majestic dream'. Leigh Hunt wrote of 'Kubla Khan' as 'a piece of the invisible world made visible by sun at moonlight and sliding before the eyes' while Algernon Swinburne claimed that in the same poem 'An exquisite instinct married to a subtle science of verse has made it the supreme model of music in our language'.

There was a tendency to read Coleridge as a poet of pure music, without attending much to meanings. Hazlitt famously called 'Kubla Khan' a piece of nonsense verse. Coleridge's description of 'Kubla Khan' as 'a psychological curiosity', of *The Ancient Mariner* as a poem of 'pure **Imagination**, and his emphasis on the verse of *Christabel* as its most interesting feature persuaded most readers that they need not bother too much about interpreting these poems. Not until Walter Pater's *Appreciations* (1889) did anyone see Coleridge's visionary poems as all of a piece with his lifelong exploration of 'a spiritual, or **Platonic** view of things'. No-one cared much for, or wrote much about the conversation poems. Swinburne said Coleridge's **blank verse** poems were 'mostly in an embryonic state, with birthmarks on them of debility or malformation'. Coleridge himself was in fact very diffident about his blank verse poems. He published one of them in 1796 with the subtitle 'A poem which affects not to be poetry'. Parts of the conversation poems, he felt, were 'too tame even for animated prose'.

FURTHER READING

Alun R. Jones and William Tydeman, eds. *Coleridge: The Ancient Mariner and Other Poems*. A Casebook, Macmillan, 1973; J. R. de J. Jackson, *Coleridge: The Critical Heritage*, Routledge & Kegan Paul, 1970.

THE REPUTATION OF *CHRISTABEL*

Christabel is a convenient text with which to illustrate the development of Coleridge criticism towards interpretation. Nineteenth-century readers were content to like or dislike it. Perhaps inspired by rumours of one of the poem's projected endings, in which Geraldine ceases to appear in the form of the daughter of Roland de Vaux and adopts instead the form of Christabel's absent lover, William Hazlitt circulated the rumour that Geraldine was really a man in disguise. More publicly he declared in his 1818 review, 'there is something disgusting at the bottom of his subject, which is but ill glossed over by a veil of Della Cruscan sentiment and fine writing – like moonbeams playing on a charnel house'. Yet Lord Byron referred to it twice as 'a wild and singularly beautiful and original poem' and added his voice to those who called for its publication, while Swinburne found it the 'loveliest' of Coleridge's poems, imbued with 'inner and outer sweetness': 'The very terror and mystery of magical evil is imbued with this sweetness; the witch has no less of it than the maiden; their contact has nothing dissonant or disfiguring, nothing to jar or to deface the beauty of the whole imagination'.

    One of the most influential of modern readings of *Christabel* is that of the poet and critic Charles Tomlinson, who sees *Christabel* as 'perhaps the only tale of terror which expresses with any real subtlety the basic pattern of the genre'. In his essay (in the Macmillan Casebook) Christabel is in the position of the typical persecuted woman of the **Gothic** tale, but her predicament is explored through symbolic rather than narrative means, and it is through symbolic means that Coleridge renders the horror of Geraldine apparently coveting Christabel's identity, and Christabel unconsciously assuming Geraldine's. Others have argued that *Christabel* consciously deconstructs the gender bias of Gothic, and is centred on the cruel domination and marginalisation of women by patriarchy: in this approach the treatment of both Christabel and Geraldine, by Sir Leoline, Bard Bracy and the narrator are seen as self-consciously dramatising the silencing of women and the distortion of their experience by 'male language'.

On the problem of why Coleridge did not finish *Christabel*, Charles Lamb took the view that any conclusion could only be a disappointing unravelling of a perfectly wrought sense of mystery. Modern readers have wanted explanations, which have ranged from Geoffrey Yarlott's explanation that the subject matter of the poem was too close to Coleridge's own domestic situation, to Anthony Harding's view that narrative completion is irrelevant: the poem is, in effect, a complete examination of a soul caught in a state of prayerlessness, and the 'characters' in the poem symbolise a 'Christabel-element', or a 'Geraldine element', a 'Leoline-element' a 'Bracy-element' in the human psyche. Dennis Welch has claimed that the poem founders on Coleridge's inability to handle the exceptionally difficult topic of father-daughter sexual abuse. Christabel, in this reading, bears all the classic marks of sexual abuse by her father, whose castle represents the Gothic citadel of patriarchy, and Geraldine is as likely to be the victim of the baron's own soldiers as of anyone else.

FURTHER READING

Anthony Harding, 'Mythopoesis: the unity of *Christabel*', in Gravil, Newlyn and Roe, eds, *Coleridge's Imagination*, Cambridge University Press, 1985; Karen Swann, 'Teaching Christabel: Gender and Genre', in Richard E Matlak, ed., *Approaches to Teaching Coleridge's Poetry and Prose*, Modern Language Association of America, 1991; Dennis M. Welch, 'Coleridge's Christabel: A/version of a Family Romance', *Women's Studies*, Volume 21 (1992) pp. 163–84; Geoffrey Yarlott, *Coleridge and the Abyssinian Maid*, Methuen, 1967.

Coleridge's interpreters in the twentieth century have been scholars of immense learning, intent to track Coleridge in his voluminous reading. J. Livingston Lowes produced an early classic of literary detection in his monumental *The Road to Xanadu* (Constable, 1927) in which he basically accounted for *The Ancient Mariner* and 'Kubla Khan' in terms of Coleridge's accumulated reading in antiquarian volumes, works of travel and philosophy. John Beer has to some extent followed in that vein, but making subtler and more imaginative use of the whole range of Coleridge's religious, philosophical and mythological investigations in order to plumb Coleridge's symbolism. Thomas McFarland provided the most focused investigation of exactly where Coleridge stood in the conflict between religion and philosophy, in a book which combines a challenging intellectual narrative with learned excursus notes on the entire relevant philosophical tradition, while Raimonda Modiano focuses on the origins and specificities of Coleridge's nature philosophy.

Before the modern recovery of the political contexts of Romanticism set in, Rene Wellek concluded in an essay called 'Romanticism Re-Examined' that most contributors to the modern attempt to define Romanticism see 'the implication of imagination, symbol, myth, and organic nature' as part of the attempt to 'overcome the split' between the self and the world. A major problem with this reading, of Romanticism in general and Coleridge in particular, was that it says little about the politics of the writers. For a contemporary of the Romantics, like William Hazlitt, the poetry of the Romantics was the literary equivalent of the French Revolution: a primarily democratic event. M. H. Abrams accounts for this in what is perhaps the classic exposition of modern attempts to read Romanticism as a mythic undertaking. Abrams reads all the major works of Romanticism as attempts to restate in secular and naturalistic terms the Judaeo-Christian figuring of human life as a cycle of innocence, fall and redemption, attempts in which early political efforts at restoring an unfallen world become sublimated – after the 'failure' of the French Revolution – into an imaginative apocalypse.

Further Reading

M. H. Abrams, *Natural Supernaturalism*, Oxford University Press, 1971; John Beer, *Coleridge the Visionary*, Chatto & Windus, 1959 and

Coleridge's Poetic Intelligence, Macmillan, 1977; J. Robert Barth, S.J., *Coleridge and Christian Doctrine*, Fordham University Press, 1969; J. Livingston Lowes, *The Road to Xanadu*, Constable, 1927; Thomas McFarland, *Coleridge and the Pantheist Tradition*, Oxford University Press, 1969; Raimonda Modiano, *Coleridge and the Concept of Nature*, Macmillan, 1985; Rene Wellek, *Concepts of Criticism*, Yale University Press, 1963.

RECENT REASSESSMENTS

Recent work on Coleridge and on Romanticism generally has been concerned to resist what has become known as Romantic '**ideology**', and to examine Romanticism from a standpoint sceptical of its own claims and self-constructions. Such scepticism has become particularly marked in **New Historicist** approaches to the poetry. Whereas most historical approaches to Romantic poetry (such as Carl Woodring, Kelvin Everest and Nicholas Roe) are content to illuminate the historical contexts in which the poet worked, especially the relation between his work and that of close associates in radical dissenting circles, New Historicism has shown a more 'deconstructive' tendency. That is, rather than taking the ideals and conscious opinions of the poets at face value, New Historicism examines the unconscious historicity of texts, seeing the poets as products of history rather than as free agents within history. The emphasis of such criticism tends to be on indicating how, willy nilly, the bourgeois Romantic poet is a representative of class interests and assumptions, and far from enhancing consciousness is a purveyor of false consciousness. Thus in the writings of Jerome McGann and Marilyn Butler, Coleridge is an agent of 'German ideology', helping to snuff out the radical materialism of the French Enlightenment. Patrick Keane's work also sniffs out unconscious racism and imperialism in Coleridge's work, while showing how *The Ancient Mariner* reflects contemporary events such as the treason trials of 1794 and anti-slavery agitation. A side effect of New Historicism is the generation of surprising new readings based upon 'absence', or what is not said in texts. In two contrary ways, for instance, 'Kubla Khan' can be read as a poem about the failure of the French Revolution: either because the dome is an ideal, rationalist, construction brought down by anarchic energies, to which the poetic response – like Romanticism as a whole – is a new paradise of the imagination; or, contrariwise, because Coleridge finds in himself secret sympathies with the threatened potentate who has at least imposed momentary order on chaos, and like the poet, is in 'retirement' from public turmoil.

The obvious signs of misogyny in Coleridge (he once wrote to his wife that 'in sex, acquirements, and in the quantity and quality of natural endowments, whether of feeling or of intellect, you are the inferior') have led to surprisingly few **feminist** broadsides, perhaps because he was praising the intellectual qualities of Sara Hutchinson at about the same time. Naturally the representation of women in *The Ancient Mariner*, *Christabel* and 'Kubla Khan' (one woman 'wailing for her demon lover', the other a 'damsel with a dulcimer') has struck critics as aligned to somewhat suspect stereotypes. There is some evidence that Coleridge wished to see women as equals (he admired Mary Wollstonecraft and Dorothy Wordsworth, and relied upon Sara Hutchinson as a collaborator) even though his poetry tends to represent women as silent objects of desire or loathing. Women writers on Coleridge (from his daughter and first editor, Sara Coleridge, to Kathleen Coburn the lead editor of his Notebooks) have been remarkably forgiving. Interesting arguments have been offered by Anya Taylor to suggests that Coleridge, intellectually at least, assented to very progressive estimates of women's powers. Coleridge features in Anne Mellor's *Romanticism and Gender* (1993), however, as one poet who characteristically appropriates, indeed monopolises, whatever of the feminine he finds valuable – for instance the 'feminine' qualities of sympathetic imagination and tenderness – but can only represent actual females as silent (Sara in 'The Eolian Harp'), as victim (Christabel), as demonic (the nightmare Life-in-Death) or perverted (Geraldine).The intelligence of the real Mrs Coleridge comes out in Molly Lefebure's *The Bondage of Love: a life of Mrs Coleridge* (Gollancz, 1986).

FURTHER READING
Marilyn Butler, *Romantics, Rebels and Reactionaries*, Oxford University Press, 1981; Kelvin Everest, *Coleridge's Secret Ministry*, Harvester Press, 1979; Patrick J. Keane, *Coleridge's Submerged Politics: The Ancient Mariner and Robinson Crusoe*, University of Missouri Press, 1994; Jerome

McGann, *The Romantic Ideology*, University of Chicago Press, 1983; Anne K. Mellor, *Romanticism and Gender*, Routledge, 1993; Nicholas Roe, *Wordsworth and Coleridge: the Radical Years*, Clarendon Press, 1988; Anya Taylor, 'Coleridge, Wollstonecraft and the Rights of Women', in Tim Fulford and Morton Paley, eds. *Coleridge's Visionary Languages*, D. S. Brewer, 1993; Carl Woodring, *Politics in the Poetry of Coleridge*, University of Wisconsin Press, 1961.

POET TO POET

The most exciting recent writing on Coleridge is that of Ted Hughes, the late poet laureate. In two major essays in *Winter Pollen* (Faber & Faber, 1994) Coleridge is presented as struggling throughout his major poetry with what Hughes sees as the demands of the culturally repressed pagan Goddess. In a sense Hughes confirms the nineteenth century's judgement that the essential poems are 'Kubla Khan', *The Ancient Mariner* and *Christabel*, but in a far deeper and more challenging context. First he recognises in the demonic energies of the verse in these three poems a progressive liberation from the alien system of metre, culminating in the accentual music of *Christabel*, where an ancient music imposes itself on ordinary language like an eruption of primal energies, raising it to dance.

More importantly, the three poems amount, in Hughes's reading, to a tragic drama. In 'Kubla Khan' – the overture and first act – Coleridge briefly surrenders himself to the Abyssinian priestess, becoming transformed at the end of the poem into the 'demon lover' called for at the start. In *The Ancient Mariner* (Act 2 of the drama) the Mariner whose slaying of the Albatross is really a crucifixion of the Goddess in bird form, performs blood sacrifice to the Goddess (when he bites his arm and drinks his own blood). In consequence, he is granted a blissful realisation of the beauty of that which his Christian consciousness has previously rejected as loathsome. In *Christabel* (Act 3), Geraldine manifests her power in temporarily raising both Christabel and Sir Leoline from their respectively repressed and morbid conditions into an ecstatic one. In each 'Act' of this drama we see the call of the female to the pagan self, and her offer of the gift of song (as in the Mariner's

strange power of speech) but in each case the 'Christian' self ends in
rejecting that call. Thus, in 'Kubla Khan' Coleridge's Christian mind has
the last word: 'Beware! Beware!' and in Part 2 of *Christabel* the
Christianised Bard offers to exorcise the dark forest with holy song.
What *Christabel* voices in Coleridge, Hughes argues, is an 'unleavened
self' – resistant to prayer – which is wholly at odds with his moralistic
Christian self, and his renunciation of poetry is a refusal to explore the
implications of that self.

FURTHER READING
Ted Hughes, 'Myths, Metres, Rhythms', and 'The Snake in the Oak',
Winter Pollen: Occasional Prose, ed. William Scammell, Faber & Faber,
1994, pp. 310–465.

FURTHER READING

BIOGRAPHY
W. J. Bate, *Coleridge*, Weidenfeld and Nicolson, 1969
> A still classic literary biography

Richard Holmes, *Coleridge: Early Visions*, Hodder & Stoughton, 1989
> A genial biography, made especially vivid (if somewhat uncritical) by drawing
> extensively on Coleridge's own words

Molly Lefebure, *Samuel Taylor Coleridge: a Bondage of Opium*. Victor
Gollancz, 1974
> A fascinating account of Coleridge's battle against 'a truly fearful bondage'

CRITICISM
George Dekker, *Coleridge and the Literature of Sensibility*, Vision Press,
1978
> A major reassessment of the genesis and meaning of Coleridge's 'dejection' poems

Robert Penn Warren, 'A poem of Pure Imagination,' in *Selected Essays*,
Eyre & Spottiswoode, 1964
> A classic essay on the symbolism of *The Ancient Mariner*

Basil Willey, *Samuel Taylor Coleridge*, Chatto & Windus, 1972
> A reader-friendly study of Coleridge's philosophical and religious work

CRITICAL ANTHOLOGIES

M. H. Abrams, ed., *English Romantic Poets*, 2nd edition, Oxford University Press, 1975

> Contains three major essays on Romanticism and four on Coleridge's poems, including G.M. Harper on the conversation poems and Humphrey House on *The Ancient Mariner*

Kathleen Coburn, ed., *Coleridge: A Collection of Critical Essays*, Twentieth Century Views, Prentice-Hall, 1967

> This excellent collection includes A. S. Gerard's still influential essay 'The Systolic Rhythm: the structure of Coleridge's Conversation Poems'

Richard Gravil, Lucy Newlyn & Nicholas Roe, eds., *Coleridge's Imagination*, Cambridge University Press, 1985

> Especially useful for Anthony John Harding's reading of the unity of *Christabel*, and John Beer's unravelling of the layers of language in 'Kubla Khan'

Richard Gravil & Molly Lefebure, eds., *The Coleridge Connection*, Macmillan, 1990

> A collaborative study of Coleridge's friendships and connections, which includes Nicholas Roe on Coleridge and Thelwall, Molly Lefebure on the chemist Humphry Davy, and James Engell on Coleridge and German Idealism

Alun R. Jones & William Tydeman, eds., *Coleridge: The Ancient Mariner and Other Poems*, Casebook Series, Macmillan, 1973

> Reprints six stimulating essays on *The Ancient Mariner*, 'Kubla Khan' and *Christabel*

World events	Author's life	Literary events
1770 Cook discovers Australia		**1770** Thomas Chatterton, poet, dies aged 18; Oliver Goldsmith *The Deserted Village;* William Wordsworth born
	1772 Samuel Taylor Coleridge born, Ottery St Mary, Devon, tenth child of the Rev. John Coleridge and his second wife, Ann Bowdon	
	1774 Attends Dame School	**1774** Goethe, *The Sorrows of Young Werther*
1775 American War of Independence begins	**1775** At age of three, can read Bible	
		1776 David Hume, philosopher, dies
1778 Britain declares war on France which has allied with American Colonists		
	1779 Attends Henry VIII Free Grammar School, where father is a master; discovers *Arabian Nights' Entertainments*	
1781 William Pitt enters Parliament	**1781** Father dies of a heart attack	**1781** Immanuel Kant, *Critique of Pure Reason*
	1782 Becomes boarder at Christ's Hospital School, London	**1782** Rousseau, *Confessions*
1783 American Colonies' independence recognised; Pitt's first ministry		
1786 Mont Blanc climbed for first time		
1788 George III's first attack of madness		
1789 French Revolution begins; Declaration of the Rights of Man; fall of La Bastille		**1789** William Blake, *Songs of Innocence*

World events	Author's life	Literary events
	1790 Ill with jaundice and rheumatic fever	**1790** Edmund Burke, *Reflections on the Revolution in France*
	1791 Scholarship to Jesus College, Cambridge	**1791** Thomas Paine, *The Rights of Man*
1792 France becomes a Republic		**1792** Mary Wollstonecraft, *A Vindication of the Rights of Woman*
1793 France and Britain at war;execution of Louis XVI; Reign of Terror	**1793** Enlists in Dragoons	**1793** William Godwin, *Inquiry Concerning Political Justice*; Wordsworth, *Descriptive Sketches*
1794 Joseph Priestley emigrates to America (after rioters burn his laboratory); John Thelwall and other Jacobins tried for treason	**1794** Returns to Cambridge; walking tour; meets Southey; becomes engaged to Southey's fiancée's sister Sara; plans to establish Utopian community; Southey and Coleridge, *The Fall of Robespierre* (play); *Monody on the Death of Chatterton*; Coleridge and Southey plan to emigrate to America	**1794** Blake, *The Book of Urizen*; *Songs of Experience*
1795-9 France governed by Directoire	**1795** Moves to Bristol; marries Sara; meets Wordsworth; political lectures and Anti-Slavery lecture in Bristol	
	1796 Publishes *The Watchman*; Hartley born; moves to Nether Stowey	
	1797 Begins *The Rime of the Ancient Mariner*; friendship with Wordsworth	
	1798 With Wordsworth, *Lyrical Ballads*; Josiah Wedgewood offers Coleridge annuity of £150; Berkeley born	
	1799 With Wordsworths in Germany; Berkeley dies; falls in love with Sara Hutchinson	**1799** Schiller, *Wallenstein*

World events	Author's life	Literary events
1800 Napoleon defeats Austria in Battle of Marengo	**1800** Derwent born; Coleridge moves to Keswick; with Wordsworth excludes *Christabel* from *Lyrical Ballads*	**1800** Wordsworths move to Grasmere; William Cowper dies; Maria Edgeworth, *Castle Rackrent*
1802 Peace of Amiens	**1802** Sara born	
1803 Britain renews war with France		
1804 Napoleon becomes Emperor; younger Pitt Prime Minister again	**1804-6** Public secretary to Governor of Malta	
1805 Battle of Trafalgar		**1805** Walter Scott, *The Lay of the Last Minstrel*; Wordsworth, first draft of *The Prelude*
	1806 Returns to London; gives course of philosophical lectures	
1807 Slave trade abolished in British Empire		
1808 Peninsular War begins	**1808** Returns to Lake District; later sharing Wordsworth's new home	**1808** Goethe, *Faust*
	1809-10 Writes and edits *The Friend* with Sara Hutchinson's help	
	1810 Back in London, writing and lecturing	**1810** Scott, *The Lady of the Lake*
		1811 Jane Austen, *Sense and Sensibility*
1812 Napoleon retreats from Moscow		**1812** Byron, *Childe Harold*
	1813 *Remorse* (play)	
		1814 Shelley, *Refutation of Deism*; Wordsworth, *The Excursion*
1815 Battle of Waterloo		**1815** Wordsworth, *Poems*
	1816 Opium addiction under control; *Christabel*, 'Kubla Khan', 'The Pains of Sleep'	

World events	Author's life	Literary events
	1817 *Sibylline Leaves; Biographia Literaria; The Statesman's Manual*	
	1818 *On Method*	**1818** Mary Shelley, *Frankenstein;* Keats, *Endymion*
1819 Peterloo Massacre		**1819** Byron, *Don Juan*
1820 George III dies, George IV accedes		**1820** Keats, *Lamia, Isabella, Eve of St Agnes*
		1821 John Keats dies; Shelley, *Adonais*
		1822 Shelley drowns; Thomas de Quincey, *Confessions of an English Opium Eater*
		1823 Carlyle, 'The Life of Schiller'; James Fenimore Cooper, *The Pioneers*
	1824 Becomes associate of Royal Society of Literature	**1824** Lord Byron dies
	1825 *Aids to Reflection*	
		1826 Cooper, *Last of the Mohicans*
	1829 American edition of *Aids to Reflection*	
1830 George IV dies; William IV accedes; Louis-Philippe becomes 'citizen king' of France	**1830** *On the Constitution of Church and State*	
		1832 Tennyson, *Poems;* Scott and Goethe die
1834 Tolpuddle Martyrs transported to Australia; slavery abolished in British Empire		**1834** Harrison Ainsworth, *Rookwood;* Carlyle, *Sartor Resartus*
	1835 Dies at Highgate	
		1836 Ralph Waldo Emerson, *Nature*
		1837 Charles Dickens, *Pickwick Papers*

accentual verse a traditional folk measure in which each line usually has four stressed syllables, however many syllables there are

allegory a narrative in which the agent or events are emblematic

alliteration the correspondence of consonants. In the line 'In Xanadu did Kubla Khan' there is triple alliteration (on n, d and k) and triple assonance (on i, a and u)

archaism the use of obsolete words or syntax of an older period, as in 'eftsoons'

assonance the correspondence of stressed vowels

ballad metre a quatrain, usually iambic, of alternating tetrameter and trimeter, rhyming *abcb* or *abab*

blank verse verse in continuous paragraphs of unrhymed iambic pentameter. It is hard to find a strictly regular example in Coleridge's poems, but 'By lákes and sándy shóres, benéath the crágs' (in 'Frost at Midnight') is one

closure an effect of completeness or finality, especially in narrative. Several of Coleridge's poems are so open-ended that it seems inappropriate to arrive at a single, or 'closed' interpretation

deism the Enlightenment belief that God is a reasonable inference from creation, and that there is no need for dogma or divine revelation

emblem an object which conveys a specific idea, sometimes arbitrarily, as in the association of the myrtle and jasmine with particular virtues in Coleridge's 'The Eolian Harp'.

The white and red rose are emblems for Lancashire and Yorkshire respectively

feminist criticism the application of feminist ideology to literary texts. Feminism argues that society is patriarchal, and that women are oppressed for the benefit of men.

Feminist critics seek to uncover the gender bias of male writers (or women writers complicit with their own oppression) as shown, for instance, in the representation of women as silent, or as deriving their value from their usefulness as domestic creatures or poetic muses

gloss explanations, usually of words (as in a glossary of terms) but sometimes of events or ideas.

The gloss printed alongside the 1817 text of *The Ancient Mariner* – and occasionally spilling across the page – is an unusually prominent example

Gothic in a general sense, anything originating, or claiming to originate from the Middle Ages, is Gothic, but the term usually implies a tale of terror, mystery and imagination, in a medieval or remote and atmospheric setting

heroic couplet lines of iambic pentameter rhymed in pairs

idealism any philosophical theory which suggests that the external world is created by the mind, or, more loosely, that all that we know of the world is ideas formed by our minds from data provided by our senses

iambic pentameter see metre and pentameter

image, imagery strictly speaking, what we 'see' when we perceive an object. But in a looser sense Blake's line 'Softest clothing, woolly bright' (in his poem 'The Lamb') contains four images: softness, clothing, woolly and brightness.

Images can be anything detected by any of the senses, or by the mind – such as imagery of disease, luxury, money, industry. Sometimes the term 'imagery' is used even more loosely to include figurative language such as simile, metaphor and symbol

Imagination and Fancy imagination is, usually, the mental faculty which forms images of absent objects, or non-existent objects. Coleridge, however, insisted that the mind is creative in all its acts of perception, and used the term **'primary imagination'** to indicate this activity.

Poets and visionaries and politicians, however, also use **'secondary imagination'**, whereby they are able to dissolve what they perceive, and recombine its elements into new forms. Also, an imaginative mind perceives or creates unity and relation. According to Coleridge the lesser activity of combining ready-made images, without changing their nature or creating such unity of impression, is merely Fancy

lyric originally intended to be sung, and usually written in stanzas (groups of lines with a fixed pattern of rhyme and metre) sometimes very complex. Lyric poetry is often exploratory or expressive of strong personal feeling

Lyrical Ballads In *Lyrical Ballads* Wordworth and Coleridge deliberately combined simple ballad metre with complex explorations of feeling as one of innumerable rebellions against traditional genre-divisions. In part their choice of ballad form for some major statements is a democratic choice, a deliberate identification with the people. At the same time they saw the connection between ballad metre and the resources of ritual and myth

metaphor a compressed simile and nowadays often applied to both. Burns saying that 'My love *is like* a red, red rose / That's newly sprung in June' is making a simile. Metaphor fuses the image with its content: Wordsworth's Lucy *is* 'a violet by a mossy stone/half hidden from the eye'. In fact both are using a flower to express a specific quality or qualities of the real subject – her freshness or shyness, hiddenness and rootedness

metre poetic metre divides lines into 'feet'. A line can be made up of any number of feet from one to eight. Feet are regular units of two syllables (duple metre) or three syllables (triple meter). The duple metres are represented by the accents in such names as Berlín (iamb, iambic), Lóndon (trochee, trochaic), Néw Yórk (spondee, spondaic). The commonest triple metres are Éxeter (dactyl, dactylic), Teneríife (anapaest, anapaestic)

Millennium as used by Coleridge, the thousand-year reign of Christ and his Saints which follows the catastrophic events of the **apocalypse** and prophesied as preceding the Last Judgement

New Historicism a critical method designed to uncover historical determinants which are not immediately apparent in texts, or which the text appears to transcend

ode a complex lyric poem, characterised by intricate stanza forms, and seriousness of purpose. The most elaborate form of ode was invented by the Greek poet Pindar, and a simpler form by the Latin poet Horace

one Life, the Coleridge's phrase for the unity of living things – divine, human, animal, vegetable

organic form, organicism Coleridge promoted the idea that poetry should create its own form, as it unfolds, like a plant, rather than follow a mechanical form, imposed on the material

Pantheism and Panentheism strictly speaking, Pantheism identifies God with Creation. That is, it denies a transcendent, personal God. With that denial goes a denial of the Trinity, and the doctrines of Incarnation and Redemption. So Pantheism is incompatible with Christianity. Panentheism also sees the universe as the divine substance, but holds that God can be both immanent and transcendent. Coleridge might reasonably claim that even in the poems which seem pantheist he is really Panentheist

paradox an apparent contradiction or yoking together of opposites in an extreme antithesis

y

pentameter a poetic line of five feet, not necessarily **iambic**, but most often so

Platonism and Neoplatonism Plato, the Greek philosopher (born 428BC) was the founder of philosophical idealism, and also profoundly influenced Christian thought. He believed that nothing in the material world is permanent, or 'Real'. Knowledge, therefore, is derived not from the senses but from reason. The Neoplatonist Plotinus (AD204–70) thought the visible world was the creation of a sort of cosmic Soul; it was beautiful and (as in the gloss to *The Ancient Mariner*) inhabited by spirits. From St Augustine (345–430) onwards, Christian thought was largely built on Plotinus's representation of Plato's ideas

poetic diction the kind of language employed by poets of the eighteenth century who felt that poetry should employ an elevated and often rather outmoded vocabulary, such as 'zephyr' for breeze, 'verdant herb' for grass, 'feathery tribes' for birds. Wordsworth provocatively used a deliberately homely style in many of his poems, as part of a democratisation of poetry

quatrain a stanza of four lines, or a four-line section within a larger structure

Reason Coleridge, following Immanuel Kant, distinguishes this term from Understanding. Coleridge's 'Reason' denotes the faculty which apprehends truths unamenable to empirical thought. The calculating Reason despised by William Blake, and the 'consequitive reasoning' which Keats thought unlikely to arrive at any fresh insight unless guided by Imagination, are in Coleridge's more philosophical vocabulary, 'Understanding'

rhetoric strictly, the art of persuasive speaking or writing; loosely, the use of artificially heightened language

rhyme identity of final vowel (and consonant) in lines of verse. **Masculine rhyme** is on one syllable (feet, greet); **feminine rhyme** on two (bellow, yellow)

satire a work designed to expose someone or something to ridicule

scriptible a term used by the French critic Roland Barthes to indicate a special kind of open-ended text that requires the reader's constant and active participation if it is to be understood. This is contrasted with the *lisible* or readable text, which can be read in a passive way. Blake, Wordsworth, Coleridge and Shelley specialised in texts which require the reader to complete them and may yield nothing at all to the passive reader

septet, sestet respectively, a seven- or six-line stanza, or unit of rhyme within a larger structure, such as the last seven lines of each stanza of 'France. An Ode' or the last six lines 'Sonnet: to the River Otter'

sibilance an effect created by employing sibilants, i.e. sounds such as 's', 'sh'. Other categories of sound include **fricatives** ('f' sounds), nasals ('m' and 'n'), **plosives** ('p', 't').

simile see metaphor

sonnet a lyric poem of fourteen lines of iambic pentameter made up of almost any combination of shorter rhyme structures, such an **octave** (eight lines; usually divided into two quatrains), and a sestet (either a quatrain and a couplet or two tercets) or simply three quatrains and a couplet

stress vague term to indicate prominent syllables in poetic metre. All multi-syllabic words have a fixed 'accent' on one or more syllables (as in the noun áccent or the verb accéntuate) and poetic metre makes patterns of accented and non-accented syllables. 'Stress' can mean length (mean has a long vowel, length a short one), increased volume, or a change of pitch. Excited, angry or threatening speech can be crowded with stress

strophe strictly, a unit of Greek choral song, or a choric section in a Pindaric ode. In this Note I use the term for the sections of 'Dejection: An Ode' which are irregular (and therefore not stanzas) and rhymed (and therefore more formal than 'verse paragraphs')

sublime / sublimity a sublime experience elevates the soul or expands the mind. In classical literature sublimity was associated with the contemplation of heroes and gods. In Romanticism it is more often associated with awe-inspiring natural scenery, such as immense heights or depths – especially indefinite ones – which inspire a sense of one's insignificance, followed by a compensatory feeling in which the mind recognises its own immensity

tetrameter and trimeter poetic lines of four and three metrical 'feet' respectively

Unitarian a Christian who believes that God is One, that Christ was not divine, but the great mediator between God and man, that the world is a manifestation of God, and that all human beings are to be saved. Conversely, Unitarians reject the doctrine of the Trinity (i.e. that God is 'father, son and holy ghost'), the idea of the crucifixion as atonement (God's self-sacrifice, by which man is redeemed), the notion that some are predestined to eternal punishment, and the idea that spirit is good and matter (including nature) is 'fallen'. Along with these ideas Unitarians, like Baptists and other 'dissenters' held very democratic and egalitarian political ideas. They were in the forefront of English radicalism from the American revolution (1776) through to the 1830s

Richard Gravil is Reader in English and American Literature at The College of St Mark and St John, Plymouth. He has co-edited two collections of critical essays on Coleridge, *Coleridge's Imagination* (1985) and *The Coleridge Connection* (1990). His forthcoming work includes *Romantic Dialogues: Anglo-American Continuities, 1776–1862* (St Martin's Press, 2000), and *Master Narratives: Tellers and Telling in the English Novel* (Scolar Press, 2000).

York Notes Advanced

Margaret Atwood
The Handmaid's Tale

Jane Austen
Mansfield Park

Jane Austen
Persuasion

Jane Austen
Pride and Prejudice

Alan Bennett
Talking Heads

William Blake
Songs of Innocence and of Experience

Charlotte Brontë
Jane Eyre

Emily Brontë
Wuthering Heights

Geoffrey Chaucer
The Franklin's Tale

Geoffrey Chaucer
General Prologue to the Canterbury Tales

Geoffrey Chaucer
The Wife of Bath's Prologue and Tale

Joseph Conrad
Heart of Darkness

Charles Dickens
Great Expectations

John Donne
Selected Poems

George Eliot
The Mill on the Floss

F. Scott Fitzgerald
The Great Gatsby

E.M. Forster
A Passage to India

Brian Friel
Translations

Thomas Hardy
The Mayor of Casterbridge

Thomas Hardy
Tess of the d'Urbervilles

Seamus Heaney
Selected Poems from Opened Ground

Nathaniel Hawthorne
The Scarlet Letter

James Joyce
Dubliners

John Keats
Selected Poems

Christopher Marlowe
Doctor Faustus

Arthur Miller
Death of a Salesman

Toni Morrison
Beloved

William Shakespeare
Antony and Cleopatra

William Shakespeare
As You Like It

William Shakespeare
Hamlet

William Shakespeare
King Lear

William Shakespeare
Measure for Measure

William Shakespeare
The Merchant of Venice

William Shakespeare
Much Ado About Nothing

William Shakespeare
Othello

William Shakespeare
Romeo and Juliet

William Shakespeare
The Tempest

William Shakespeare
The Winter's Tale

Mary Shelley
Frankenstein

Alice Walker
The Color Purple

Oscar Wilde
The Importance of Being Earnest

Tennessee Williams
A Streetcar Named Desire

John Webster
The Duchess of Malfi

W.B. Yeats
Selected Poems

Chinua Achebe
Things Fall Apart

Edward Albee
Who's Afraid of Virginia Woolf?

Margaret Atwood
Cat's Eye

Jane Austen
Emma

Jane Austen
Northanger Abbey

Jane Austen
Sense and Sensibility

Samuel Beckett
Waiting for Godot

Robert Browning
Selected Poems

Robert Burns
Selected Poems

Angela Carter
Nights at the Circus

Geoffrey Chaucer
The Merchant's Tale

Geoffrey Chaucer
The Miller's Tale

Geoffrey Chaucer
The Nun's Priest's Tale

Samuel Taylor Coleridge
Selected Poems

Daniel Defoe
Moll Flanders

Daniel Defoe
Robinson Crusoe

Charles Dickens
Bleak House

Charles Dickens
Hard Times

Emily Dickinson
Selected Poems

Carol Ann Duffy
Selected Poems

George Eliot
Middlemarch

T.S. Eliot
The Waste Land

T.S. Eliot
Selected Poems

Henry Fielding
Joseph Andrews

E.M. Forster
Howards End

John Fowles
The French Lieutenant's Woman

Robert Frost
Selected Poems

Elizabeth Gaskell
North and South

Stella Gibbons
Cold Comfort Farm

Graham Greene
Brighton Rock

Thomas Hardy
Jude the Obscure

Thomas Hardy
Selected Poems

Joseph Heller
Catch-22

Homer
The Iliad

Homer
The Odyssey

Gerard Manley Hopkins
Selected Poems

Aldous Huxley
Brave New World

Kazuo Ishiguro
The Remains of the Day

Ben Jonson
The Alchemist

Ben Jonson
Volpone

James Joyce
A Portrait of the Artist as a Young Man

Philip Larkin
Selected Poems

D.H. Lawrence
The Rainbow

D.H. Lawrence
Selected Stories

D.H. Lawrence
Sons and Lovers

D.H. Lawrence
Women in Love

John Milton
Paradise Lost Bks I & II

John Milton
Paradise Lost Bks IV & IX

Thomas More
Utopia

Sean O'Casey
Juno and the Paycock

George Orwell
Nineteen Eighty-four

John Osborne
Look Back in Anger

Wilfred Owen
Selected Poems

Sylvia Plath
Selected Poems

Alexander Pope
Rape of the Lock and other poems

Ruth Prawer Jhabvala
Heat and Dust

Jean Rhys
Wide Sargasso Sea

William Shakespeare
As You Like It

William Shakespeare
Coriolanus

William Shakespeare
Henry IV Pt 1

William Shakespeare
Henry V

William Shakespeare
Julius Caesar

William Shakespeare
Macbeth

William Shakespeare
Measure for Measure

William Shakespeare
A Midsummer Night's Dream

William Shakespeare
Richard II

William Shakespeare
Richard III

William Shakespeare
Sonnets

William Shakespeare
The Taming of the Shrew

William Shakespeare
Twelfth Night

William Shakespeare
The Winter's Tale

George Bernard Shaw
Arms and the Man

George Bernard Shaw
Saint Joan

Muriel Spark
The Prime of Miss Jean Brodie

John Steinbeck
The Grapes of Wrath

John Steinbeck
The Pearl

Tom Stoppard
Arcadia

Tom Stoppard
Rosencrantz and Guildenstern are Dead

Jonathan Swift
Gulliver's Travels and The Modest Proposal

Alfred, Lord Tennyson
Selected Poems

W.M. Thackeray
Vanity Fair

Virgil
The Aeneid

Edith Wharton
The Age of Innocence

Tennessee Williams
Cat on a Hot Tin Roof

Tennessee Williams
The Glass Menagerie

Virginia Woolf
Mrs Dalloway

Virginia Woolf
To the Lighthouse

William Wordsworth
Selected Poems

Metaphysical Poets